The Berlin Wall: The History and Legacy of the Wor Wall

By Charles River Editors

Edward Valachovic's picture of the Berlin Wall in 1975

About Charles River Editors

Charles River Editors provides superior editing and original writing services across the digital publishing industry, with the expertise to create digital content for publishers across a vast range of subject matter. In addition to providing original digital content for third party publishers, we also republish civilization's greatest literary works, bringing them to new generations of readers via ebooks.

Sign up here to receive updates about free books as we publish them, and visit Our Kindle Author Page to browse today's free promotions and our most recently published Kindle titles.

Introduction

East German workers building the Berlin Wall

The Berlin Wall

"From Stettin in the Baltic to Trieste in the Adriatic an 'Iron Curtain' has descended across the continent. Behind that line lie all the capitals of the ancient states of Central and Eastern Europe. Warsaw, Berlin, Prague, Vienna, Budapest, Belgrade, Bucharest and Sofia; all these famous cities and the populations around them lie in what I must call the Soviet sphere, and all are subject, in one form or another, not only to Soviet influence but to a very high and in some cases increasing measure of control from Moscow." – Winston Churchill, 1946

"Here in Berlin, one cannot help being aware that you are the hub around which turns the wheel of history. ... If ever there were a people who should be constantly sensitive to their destiny, the people of Berlin, East and West, should be they." - Martin Luther King, Jr.

"This is a historic day. East Germany has announced that, starting immediately, its borders are open to everyone. The GDR is opening its borders ... the gates in the Berlin Wall stand open." – German anchorman Hans Joachim Friedrichs

In the wake of World War II, the European continent was devastated, and the conflict left the Soviet Union and the United States as uncontested superpowers. This ushered in over 45 years of the Cold War, and a political alignment of Western democracies against the Communist Soviet bloc that produced conflicts pitting allies on each sides fighting, even as the American and Soviet militaries never engaged each other.

Though it never got "hot," the Cold War was a tense era until the dissolution of the USSR, and nothing symbolized the split more than the Berlin Wall, which literally divided the city. Berlin had been a flashpoint even before World War II ended, and the city was occupied by the different Allies even as the close of the war turned them into adversaries. After the Soviets' blockade of West Berlin was prevented by the Berlin Airlift, the Eastern Bloc and the Western powers continued to control different sections of the city, and by the 1960s, East Germany was pushing for a solution to the problem of an enclave of freedom within its borders. West Berlin was a haven for highly-educated East Germans who wanted freedom and a better life in the West, and this "brain drain" was threatening the survival of the East German economy.

In order to stop this, access to the West through West Berlin had to be cut off, so in August 1961, Soviet premier Nikita Khrushchev authorized East German leader Walter Ulbricht to begin construction of what would become known as the Berlin Wall. The wall, begun on Sunday August 13, would eventually surround the city, in spite of global condemnation, and the Berlin Wall itself would become the symbol for Communist repression in the Eastern Bloc. It also ended Khrushchev's attempts to conclude a peace treaty among the Four Powers (the Soviets, the Americans, the United Kingdom, and France) and the two German states.

The wall would serve as a perfect photo-opportunity for two presidents (Kennedy and Reagan) to hammer the Soviet Communists and their repression, but the Berlin Wall would stand for nearly 30 years, isolating the East from the West. It is estimated about 200 people would die trying to cross the wall to defect to the West.

The Cold War showed no signs of stopping throughout the 1970s and 1980s. In 1979, the Soviet Union invaded Afghanistan to support a failing communist government. The United States at first opposed the invasion only diplomatically, by refusing to participate in the 1980 Olympics in Moscow and taking various other diplomatic measures. Eventually, however, the United States began to support insurgents fighting the communist regime in Afghanistan much like the Soviet Union had done in South Vietnam years earlier. The United States and its ally Pakistan provided weapons and training to the Afghani fighters, who were able to increasingly threaten the stability of the communist regime. The Soviet Union was forced to commit more troops and resources to Afghanistan, and suffered significant casualties.

At the same time, the United States under President Reagan was engaging the Soviet Union in a large scale arms race. Reagan initially spent money trying to design an elaborate missile defense system that could intercept the Soviets' intercontinental ballistic missiles. The "Strategic Defense Initiative" was mocked as impossible and jokingly referred to as "Star Wars." But when the Soviets tried to match the United States' spending early in the decade, they badly crippled their economy.

In addition, the Soviet Union was going through a period of political instability as several aging leaders had taken the top position in the Soviet Union only to die a short period of time later. In 1985, Mikhail Gorbachev became the leader of the Soviet Union. Gorbachev came to power seeking to repair the Soviets' economy, and he took a softer stance toward the United States. The two leaders signed agreements to reduce the number of nuclear weapons and eliminate certain types of ballistic missiles. Gorbachev also reformed the Soviet Union internally, lifting restrictions on individual freedoms.

Gorbachev hoped to build the Soviet economy to relieve the persistent shortages of consumer goods it faced, which were caused by enormous military spending of the Soviet Union. Gorbachev tried to introduce some economic reforms, but they were blocked by communist hardliners. Gorbachev then came to the belief that the Soviet economy could not improved without political reform as well.

Limited political reforms, such as broadcasting uncensored debates in which politicians openly questioned government policy, backfired when they energized eastern European opposition movements which began to overthrow their communist governments in 1989. Gorbachev was unwilling to reoccupy these eastern European nations and use the Soviet army to put down these revolts.

Inspired by the revolts in Eastern Europe, the small Soviet Baltic republics, which had long chafed under Russian rule, also began to clamor for independence from the Soviet Union. In 1990, Gorbachev allowed non-Communist party politicians to run for office throughout the Soviet Union, and the Communist Party lost to independence candidates in six Soviet republics, including the three Baltic republics. The Baltic republics then declared independence from the Soviet Union.

Things came to a head in 1989. With rapid change throughout Europe, the wall faced a challenge it could not contain, the challenge of democracy's spread. On the night of November 9, 1989, the Berlin Wall was effectively removed from the midst of the city it so long divided —removed with pick axes and sledgehammers, but also removed from the hearts and minds of the people on both sides who only hours before had thought the wall's existence insurmountable. As one writer put it, "No border guard, no wall, can forever shield repressive regimes from the power of subversive ideas, from the lure of freedom."

The fall of the Berlin Wall is often considered the end of the Cold War, and the following month both President Bush and Gorbachev declared the Cold War over, but the Cold War had been thawing for most of the 1980s. President Reagan is remembered for calling the Soviet Union an "evil empire" and demanding that Gorbachev tear down the wall, but he spent the last several years of his presidency working with the Soviet leader to improve relations. The end of the Soviet Union came when Gorbachev resigned on December 25, 1991. The Soviet Union formally dissolved the next day, and the Cold War was over, with the United States outlasting its long-time adversary.

The Berlin Wall: The History and Legacy of the World's Most Notorious Wall looks at the history that led to the rise and fall of the Berlin Wall. Along with pictures of important people, places, and events, you will learn about the Berlin Wall like never before, in no time at all.

The Berlin Wall: The History and Legacy of the World's Most Notorious Wall

About Charles River Editors

Introduction

Chapter 1: Berlin at the End of World War II

The events that led to the construction of the Berlin Wall began 20 years earlier during World War II. As the Soviets turned the tide against the Nazi invasion of Russia, they were able to begin advancing west toward Germany themselves, but the Soviet armies would pay dearly for the advances they made on Germany after Hitler's invasion of Russia ended in failure: "According to the Soviet Union's estimates, the Red Army's losses in the war totaled more than 11 million troops, over 100,000 aircraft, more than 300,000 artillery pieces, and 100,000 tanks and self-propelled guns".[1] Such losses, coupled with the extreme suffering that the Soviet soldiers had experienced in the years before the attack on Berlin, ensured that the thirst for revenge would be high upon arrival. Moreover, as the Soviet armies moved through Eastern Europe, they were the first to discover concentration camps and death camps, furthering their anger. The comparison of Germany's standard of living with their own was another cause of outrage, all of which encouraged the men to show no mercy: "We will take revenge…revenge for all our sufferings…It's obvious from everything we see that Hitler robbed the whole of Europe to please his Fritzies…Their shops are piled high with goods from all the shops and factories of Europe. We hate Germany and the Germans deeply. You can often see civilians lying dead in the street…But the Germans deserve the atrocities that they unleashed."[2]

Meanwhile, Germany's losses were mounting, and the Soviet armies were on the rebound, with an advantage of almost 5:1 over Germany in manpower, as well as superiority in tanks, aircraft, and artillery. Even with these major advantages, however, the race to Berlin would inflict a heavier toll on Soviet armies than they had yet seen, and with Berlin itself heavily defended by 30 mile deep defenses in multiple directions, the Soviets would eventually suffer over 100,000 lives just taking the city, along with 350,000 other casualties.

---

[1] Evans, Richard. *The Third Reich at War.* 707.
[2] Ibid., 708.

In the months leading up to the Battle of Berlin, there was a strange division amongst the German people regarding their fate. While Hitler called for the remainder of Berlin's population to take up arms and the most loyal responded to the call, many in Berlin were resigned to a seemingly inevitable defeat. In his study of Berlin in 1945, historian Antony Beevor described a city in which a grim humor had come to replace once hopeful and proud demeanors. Though humor was certainly an attempt at levity in the face of serious concerns, Germans nevertheless joked about the soon-to-arrive Russians, referring to LSR (Luftschutzraum air-raid shelters) as actually standing for "Lernt scnhell Russich" ("Learn Russian quickly").[3] In the air raid shelters, Berliners regularly found themselves in crowded conditions, waiting out the bombing raids that were taking place on a regular basis in 1944. In a city of 3 million, Beevor explained how a tightly-packed and unsanitary atmosphere became an expected part of life in Berlin. By the year's end, much of the city's beauty and a great deal of its functionality had been destroyed.

[3] Beevor, Antony. *The Fall of Berlin 1945*. New York: Penguin Books, 2003.

A picture of damage done to Berlin during a 1944 air raid

Things weren't going any better for Germany to the west either. After the successful amphibious invasion on D-Day in June 1944, the Allies began racing east toward Germany and liberating France along the way. The Allies had landed along a 50 mile stretch of French coast, and despite suffering 8,000 casualties on D-Day, over 100,000 still began the march across the western portion of the continent. By the end of August 1944, the German army in France was shattered, with 200,000 killed or wounded and a further 200,000 captured. However, Hitler reacted to the news of invasion with glee, figuring it would give the Germans a chance to destroy the Allied armies that had water to their backs. As he put it, "The news couldn't be better. We have them where we can destroy them."

While that sounds delusional in retrospect, it was Hitler's belief that by splitting the Allied march across Europe in their drive toward Germany, he could cause the collapse of the enemy armies and cut off their supply lines. Part of Hitler's confidence came as a result of underestimating American resolve, but with the Soviets racing toward Berlin from the east, this final offensive would truly be the last gasp of the German war machine, and the month long campaign was fought over a large area of the Ardennes Forest, through France, Belgium and parts of Luxembourg. From an Allied point of view, the operations were commonly referred to as the Ardennes Offensive, while the German code phrase for the operation was Unternehmen Wacht am Rhein ("Operation Watch on the Rhine"), with the initial breakout going under the name of "Operation Mist." Today, it is best known as the Battle of the Bulge.

Regardless of the term for it, and despite how desperate the Germans were, the Battle of the Bulge was a massive attack against primarily American forces that inflicted an estimated 100,000 American casualties, the heaviest American loss in any battle of the war. However, while the German forces did succeed in bending and at some points even breaking through Allied lines (thus causing the "bulge" reflected in the moniker), the Germans ultimately failed. As Winston Churchill himself said of the battle, "This is undoubtedly the greatest American battle of the war, and will, I believe be regarded as an ever famous American victory."

The end of the Battle of the Bulge led to the historic Yalta Conference between Roosevelt, Churchill, and Stalin from January 30-February 3. It was not lost on anyone present that the Allies were pushing the Nazis back on both fronts and the war in Europe was ending. The Big Three held the conference with the intention of redrawing the post-war map, but within a few years, the Cold War divided the continent anyway. As a result, Yalta became a subject of intense controversy, and to some extent, it has remained controversial. Among the agreements, the Conference called for Germany's unconditional surrender, the split of Berlin, and German demilitarization and reparations. Stalin, Churchill and Roosevelt also discussed the status of Poland, and Russian involvement in the United Nations.

The three leaders at Yalta

By this time, Stalin had thoroughly established Soviet authority in most of Eastern Europe and made it clear that he had no intention of giving up lands his soldiers had fought and died for. The best he would offer Churchill and Roosevelt was the promise that he would allow free elections to be held, but at the same time, he made clear that the only acceptable outcome to any Polish election would be one that supported communism. One Allied negotiator would later describe Stalin's very formidable negotiating skills: "Marshal Stalin as a negotiator was the toughest proposition of all. Indeed, after something like thirty years' experience of international conferences of one kind and another, if I had to pick a team for going into a conference room, Stalin would be my first choice. Of course the man was ruthless and of course he knew his purpose. He never wasted a word. He never stormed, he was seldom even irritated."

The final question was over what to do with a conquered Germany. The British, Americans and Russians all wanted Berlin, and they knew that whoever held the most of it when the truce was signed would end up controlling the city. Thus, they spent the next several months pushing their generals further and further toward this goal. Since the Russians ultimately got there first, when the victorious Allies met in Potsdam in 1945, it remained Britain and America's task to convince Stalin to divide the country, and even the city of Berlin, between them. They ultimately accomplished this, but at a terrible cost: Russia acquired the previously liberated Austria.

With the race toward Berlin in full throttle, General Dwight D. Eisenhower's Allied armies were within 200 miles of the city, but his biggest battles now took place among his allies, as he now had to deal diplomatically with Churchill, Montgomery, and French war hero Charles de Gaulle. After crossing the Rhine River, General George Patton advised Eisenhower to make haste for Berlin, and British General Bernard Montgomery was confident that they could reach Berlin before the Soviets, but Eisenhower did not think it "worth the trouble".[4] Eisenhower's forces went on to capture

400,000 prisoners on April 1st in the Ruhr, but despite his success there, not everyone agreed with Eisenhower's decision, especially Winston Churchill. In Churchill's thinking, the decision to leave the taking of Berlin to the Soviets would leave lasting trouble on the European continent, a more pressing concern for the British than for Americans an ocean away. In tension-filled exchanges, Churchill made his position clear, but President Roosevelt was ill and had no stomach for angering the Soviets. For his part, Eisenhower saw his role as a purely military one, so he refused to "trespass" into political arenas that he was under the impression had been worked out at the Tehran and Yalta conferences. In fact, Roosevelt had promised Stalin that he could enter Berlin despite the obvious threat to postwar security for the European countries, and Eisenhower wanted to avoid being a pawn in the political maneuverings of the three leaders. As a result, his major concern was to avoid as many casualties as possible in the coming weeks of the war, and if the Russians were prepared to attack and had the better opportunity to do so, it would save lives of American soldiers who would otherwise have to fight their way in from the west.[5] Eisenhower did not share his peers' (Patton and Montgomery, specifically) concerns of "arriving victorious in Berlin on top of a tank."[6]

Eventually, Eisenhower made the fateful choice not to move the American forces toward Berlin but to "hold a firm front on the Elbe" instead. In making this decision, Eisenhower left Berlin's capture to the Soviet army, and his decisions have been the cause of much debate ever since. The Allied armies in the west would thus concentrate on encircling the Ruhr Valley, the center of Germany's industry, instead of competing with the Soviets for control of the city.

[4] World War II: A 50th Anniversary History. New York: Holt, 1989.288.
[5] Humes, James C. Eisenhower and Churchill: The Partnership that Saved the World. Crown Publishing Group, 2010.
[6] Ibid.

Eisenhower

There were many concerns about the Soviet Union reaching Berlin, and all of them were understandable. Most people, especially the Germans, expected far worse treatment from Soviet conquerors than the British or Americans, especially since Hitler's attack on the Soviet Union (Operation Barbarossa) had been so unexpected that it stunned even Stalin into temporary inaction. Hitler and the Germans were going to pay dearly for the treatment that the Russians, both civilians and soldiers, had received at the hands of the German armies. Furthermore, the fear of a Soviet strategic advantage in Europe, anchored by a Soviet-controlled Berlin, loomed over both eastern and western European nations. Lastly, even if Stalin kept his word about the division of post-war Germany, allowing him unchallenged control was viewed as dangerous to a world with a weakened Britain and a United States looking to return to the isolation the Atlantic Ocean had previously provided.

Churchill and Roosevelt had always disagreed on Stalin's real motivations and limits, and Churchill needed to maintain strong ties to the Americans as the war came to a close. During one of the meetings between the three, Stalin suggested that once the German armies had been defeated, 50,000 soldiers should be executed by the conquering armies in vengeance for the losses Germany had inflicted on Europe. That suggestion horrified Churchill, who stormed out of the meeting, but Stalin followed to assure Churchill that all that had been said was in jest. Churchill had very little choice but to take Stalin at his word, but he was always far more cautious than Roosevelt when it came to trust in Stalin's judgment or word. In any case, he wrote a letter to Roosevelt after his exchange with Eisenhower in March in which he said, "I wish to place on record the complete confidence felt by His Majesty's government in General Eisenhower and our pleasure that our armies are serving under his command and our admiration of his great and shining quality, character, and personality".[7] In a note he added to Eisenhower's copy of the letter, he expressed it would grieve him to know he had pained Eisenhower with his comments but still suggested that "we should shake hands with the Russians as far east as possible."[8]

By April 17, in a meeting between Eisenhower and Churchill, the fact that the Soviet army was positioned just over 30 miles from Berlin with overpowering men, artillery, and tanks convinced Churchill that the decision to allow the Soviets to lead the attack on the city was necessary. It is important to keep in perspective that Roosevelt's death just 5 days earlier likely played a role in Churchill's willingness to give in. Churchill had spent several years negotiating with both Stalin and Roosevelt, and he may have felt that time would not allow for further discussion on the matter. Eisenhower also was under pressure to end the war in Europe as soon as

---

[7] Ibid.
[8] Ibid.

possible so that American forces and attention could be directed toward the fight against Japan. The campaign in Okinawa had just started and would last until June, and the extent of the carnage there made clear that Japan had no intention of surrendering anytime soon.

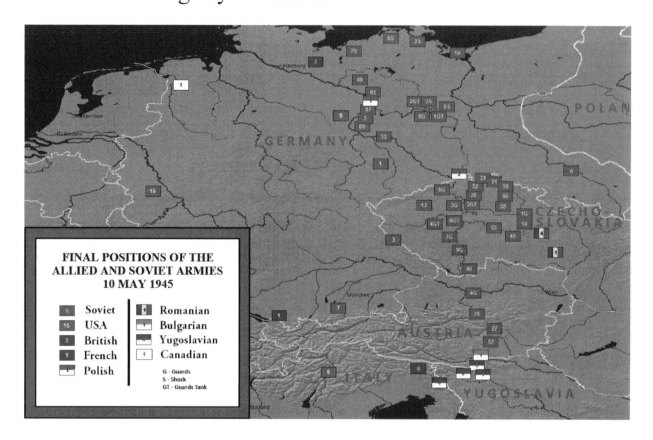

The lines at the end of World War II

The Battle of Berlin ended with an inevitable Soviet triumph, but by the time Germany officially surrendered, the Soviets had suffered over 350,000 casualties and had lost thousands of artillery batteries and armored vehicles. The Germans had suffered upwards of 100,000 dead and over 200,000 wounded, not to mention the horrors visited upon the civilian population in the wake of the battle.

With the fighting mostly coming to an end on May 2, the chain of German surrenders in the field outside of Berlin took off like dominoes. Field Marshal Wilhelm Keitel signed Germany's unconditional surrender on May 7, and news of the final surrender of the Germans was celebrated as Victory in Europe (V-E) day on May 8, 1945. Churchill delivered the following remarks to cheering crowds:

"My dear friends, this is your hour. This is not victory of a party or of any class. It's a victory of the great British nation as a whole. We were the first, in this ancient island, to draw the sword against tyranny. After a while we were left all alone against the most tremendous military power that has been seen. We were all alone for a whole year.

There we stood, alone. Did anyone want to give in? Were we down-hearted? The lights went out and the bombs came down. But every man, woman and child in the country had no thought of quitting the struggle. London can take it. So we came back after long months from the jaws of death, out of the mouth of hell, while all the world wondered. When shall the reputation and faith of this generation of English men and women fail? I say that in the long years to come not only will the people of this island but of the world, wherever the bird of freedom chirps in human hearts, look back to what we've done and they will say 'do not despair, do not yield to violence and tyranny, march straightforward and die if need be-unconquered.'"

Bundesarchiv, Bild 183-R77799
Foto: o.Ang. | 8. Mai 1945

Pictures of the Germans' unconditional surrender on May 7

Of course, the announcement of surrender was met with a far different emotion among the Germans, as one Berliner remembered: "The next day, General Wilding, the commander of the German troops in Berlin, finally surrendered the entire city to the Soviet army. There was no radio or newspaper, so vans with loudspeakers drove through the streets ordering us to cease all resistance. Suddenly, the shooting and bombing stopped and the unreal silence meant that one ordeal was over for us and another was about to begin. Our nightmare had become a reality. The entire three hundred square miles of what was left of Berlin were now completely under control of the Red Army. The last days of savage house to house fighting and street battles had been a human slaughter, with no prisoners being taken on either side. These final days were hell. Our last remaining and exhausted troops, primarily children and old men, stumbled into imprisonment. We were a city in ruins; almost no house remained intact."

The controversy over Eisenhower's decision not to press for Berlin remains, but any debate over whether the Allied armies were in a position to take Berlin must acknowledge the fact that the most significant American forces were over 200 miles from Berlin in mid-April. Nonetheless, others point to smaller American forces that were within 50 miles of the city before being told to move in the opposite direction.

The strongest critiques of Eisenhower's decisions portray him as naïve about the consequences, or as an unwitting tool of the Soviets, but his defenders call his decision "dead on".[9] Soviet casualties in taking the city rivaled those lost by the Allies at the Battle of the Bulge, and considering the earlier agreements with Stalin, General Omar Bradley believed that the Americans would have to pay "a pretty stiff price to pay for a prestige objective, especially when we've got to fall back and let the other fellow take over."[10]

---

[9] Kevin Baker, "General Discontent: Blaming Powell-And Eisenhower-For Not Having Pushed Through. (in the News)," American Heritage, November-December 2002, https://www.questia.com/read/1G1-93611493.
[10] Ibid.

Eisenhower vigorously defended himself against criticism upon his return from the war, pointing out that those who criticized his position on the issue were not the ones who would have been forced to comfort the grieving mothers of soldiers killed in an unnecessary fight to take Berlin. During his 1952 presidential campaign, he faced further criticism, and in response, he emphasized his warnings about the danger of the Soviet threat to Europe rather than discuss his decision to stay away from Berlin. Historian Stephen Ambrose saw this attempt at self-salvation by Eisenhower as wishful thinking, and that there was no evidence of Eisenhower warning against the Soviet threat to Europe during his time as general: "The truth was that he may have wished by 1952 that he had taken a hard line with the Russians in 1945, but he had not".[11]

Chapter 2: A Divided City

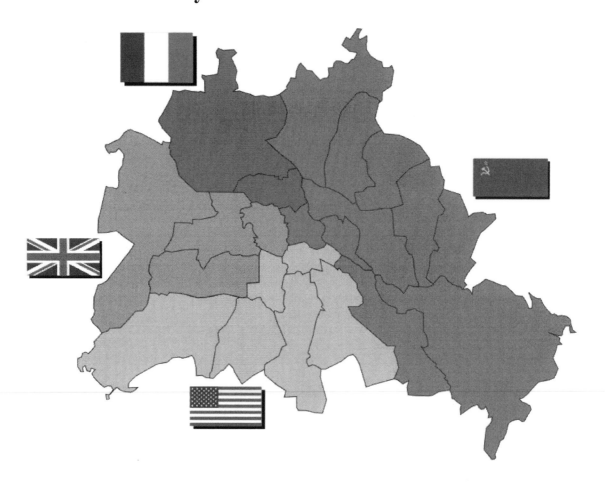

The different sections of Berlin at the end of the war

[11] Ibid.

It was a famous moment commemorated as "East Meets West" when Soviet soldiers shook hands with other Allied soldiers in Germany near the end of the war, but nobody was under any illusions that they would continue to work well together after defeating their common enemy. In 1946, speaking to a war-weary world, Winston Churchill sounded what would become a famous warning about the aggression of the Soviet Union and the dangers of communism's spread while speaking to a group of college students at Westminster College in Fulton, Missouri: "I am sure you would wish me to state the facts as I see them to you, to place before you certain facts about the present position in Europe. From Stettin in the Baltic to Trieste in the Adriatic, an iron curtain has descended across the Continent. Behind that line lie all the capitals of the ancient states of Central and Eastern Europe. Warsaw, Berlin, Prague, Vienna, Budapest, Belgrade, Bucharest and Sofia, all these famous cities and the populations around them lie in what I must call the Soviet sphere, and all are subject in one form or another, not only to Soviet influence but to a very high and, in many cases, increasing measure of control from Moscow."[12]

This "border" of states, the protection that Stalin claimed he needed to ensure his country's post-war security, included "Poland, Czechoslovakia, Hungary, Bulgaria, Romania, and the Soviet Occupation Zone in East Germany".[13] These areas would develop into Soviet satellite states, relying on the Soviet's for military defense, serving as the Soviet industrial plans' source for natural resources, and experiencing occasional crackdowns for showing signs of independence or unrest over the next 40 plus years.

At the same time, in the immediate aftermath of the war, the city of Berlin itself was divided into a French, British, American, and Soviet occupation

---

[12] Churchill, Winston. "The Sinews of Peace." Westminster College. Mississippi, Fulton. 5 Mar. 1946. *The Churchill Centre*. Web. 2 Feb. 2015.
[13] Rottman, 5.

zone. As on historian describes it, the division was uneven from the beginning: "[T]he victorious Allies unfurled a map and carved up the city - the houses then lining the south side of Bernauer Strasse wound up in the Soviet sector while the street itself and the sidewalk in front belonged to the French. By this cartographic fiat, some sectors of the population would find themselves economically rejuvenated by the Marshall Plan and reintroduced to bourgeois democratic society, while the rest were stuck with the Soviets.[14]

The city of Berlin was fully in Soviet hands between May and July of 1945, but they turned over the sectors they had agreed to back in 1944 to the British, Americans, and French. That said, in recognition of the last two months of the war, in which the Soviets had fought the Battle for Berlin at the cost of over 80,000 Soviet lives, the Soviets were given a much larger portion of the city than the rest of the Allies,[15] and as Germany divided into East and West along the borders of former German states, the city of Berlin ultimately fell well within East Germany's borders. In fact, Berlin was over 100 miles from the nearest point in what would become known as West Germany.

General Georgy Zhukov, the Soviet hero of the war, established the communist party in Berlin,[16] and the decisions governing Soviet action became immediately political, despite their desire to be seen (by both sides) as purely motivated by military necessity. At first, the city was governed by an "Allied Control Council" of the four powers, with each country rotating control on a monthly basis. In *City on Leave: A History of Berlin 1945-1962*, Philip Windsor explains that the council was marked far more for argument and conflict than true governance. In fact, he argues, "All the Western Powers were…for different reasons, convinced that collaboration with the Soviet Union in Germany was their essential task. The struggle for the country came upon them almost unawares, and at the outset none was

---

[14] Mark Ehrman, "Borders and Barriers," The Virginia Quarterly Review 83, no. 2 (2007), https://www.questia.com/read/1P3-1256577881.
[15] Ibid., 8.
[16] Philip Windsor, City on Leave: A History of Berlin, 1945-1962 (London: Chatto & Windus, 1963), 25, https://www.questia.com/read/11076907.

capable of answering the scarcely defined Russian threat. This threat would not become manifest until they were all forced to face the need of defining common economic policies and erecting a central German authority. But there was already one center in Germany where all were concerned together in a common assignation, and where the present government of the country was established. It offered a valuable, perhaps decisive, prize to Russia in the political conquest of the whole; and in the Rooseveltian terms which governed American policy, it provided the United States with the most practical test of Soviet intentions. *This was Berlin.*"[17]

---

[17] Ibid, 31. Emphasis added.

Zhukov

In the early years of the Cold War, the West seemed to be in retreat as the Soviet Union succeeded in testing its own nuclear weapon, setting up puppet states in eastern Europe, and assisting the Chinese communists in winning a civil war over Western backed Chinese nationalist forces. Stalin subsequently hoped to continue to expand Russian influence by ordering a blockade of all supplies into West Berlin, hoping the West would cede the entire city to the Soviets. However, the United States and its allies were able to organize a massive airlift of supplies that kept the city of West Berlin supplied, and the Soviet Union and its German allies eventually stopped the blockade when they realized the West could continue to supply Berlin by air indefinitely. The Berlin Airlift was one of the first major confrontations of the Cold War, but it would hardly be the last; if anything, it was just the start for the contest over Berlin.

Picture of a plane participating in the Berlin Airlift in 1948

Chapter 3: Local German Leaders

The ideological battle being played out in Berlin and greater Germany in 1961 and beforehand was fought between two spheres of influence led by the United States and the Soviet Union, but in the midst of the fight were the Germans, the people who had to live under the outcomes of policy, negotiations, and compromises formed by the push and pull of politics. Both sides of the conflict acknowledged that if the situation in Berlin ever required the use of nuclear weapons, the loss of German life would be devastating.

German leadership on both sides was required to maintain a delicate balance of working with the United States in the case of the West and the Soviets in the case of the East, as well as representing the interests and outcomes of their own people. For this reason, local leaders also played crucial roles in the division of Berlin and the construction of the wall.

Willy Brandt was the mayor of West Berlin from 1957-1966, and though he went on to serve as German chancellor and leader of a major German political party, it is for his time as mayor that he is best remembered. Brandt was a left-wing socialist who fled Germany during the Nazi reign, spending time in Scandinavia, but during the time of the Spanish Civil War, he came to distrust the Soviet Union and to champion the causes of German socialism rather than cooperation with the Soviet Union.

Brandt and Kennedy

As mayor of West Berlin, Brandt became the face for a group of over two million people whose lives hung in the balance of big decision-makers. President Kennedy invited Brandt to the White House in March 1961, and the English-speaking Brandt made a great impression on the young president. Kennedy hoped that he would be elected Chancellor of Germany in the next months, a desire that actually caused tension between Kennedy and the actual future chancellor.[18]

The future leader of communist East Germany began as a member of the Communist Party of Germany. Fleeing to Russia during the Nazi domination, Walter Ulbricht rose to power in Stalin's circles, supporting the purges and staying out of trouble. He returned to Germany as part of the Soviet occupation in 1945 and became the head of a new party, the Socialist Unity Party, which would control East Germany.[19] Ulbricht has been characterized by history as both a communist radical who pressured the Soviets into the construction of the wall, and as a leader more interested in independence and reforms that would move his country in a different direction than the other Soviet bloc nations.

Bundesarchiv, Bild 183-B0116-0010-038
Foto: Sturm, Horst | 16. Januar 1963

Ulbricht and Khrushchev

Konrad Adenauer was the first chancellor of Germany. Having been a prisoner of war under the Nazi regime, he was named the mayor of Berlin the

[18] Kempe, Frederick. "West Berlin's Impertinent Mayor". *Reuters Blog: Analysis and Opinion*. 7 June 2011.
[19] Dennis Kavanagh, ed., A Dictionary of Political Biography (Oxford: Oxford University Press, 1998), 484, https://www.questia.com/read/34683386.

day after the conclusion of the war, but the British dismissed him from this position. He formed the Christian Democratic Union party, which was anti-Socialist but concerned with the poor who had been devastated by Germany's economic hard times. Adenauer believed that friendliness with the United States, Britain, and France was necessary in order to protect Berlin and West Germany itself from the Soviets.[20]

However, Adenauer would end up being criticized by many in West Berlin for what was perceived as a lack of response to the crisis. He arrived in Berlin 9 days after the construction of the wall had begun, on August 22, 1961, and while he ultimately condemned the Soviet action, he urged the Germans to remain calm. Adenauer's defenders would point to his difficult work in receiving and negotiating with Soviet officials during the time of crisis and with saving German lives by tempering angry reactions. He certainly did not advocate West Berlin giving up their independence to the Soviet Union, as he warned, "An infallible method of conciliating a tiger is to allow oneself to be devoured."

[20] Dennis Kavanagh, ed., A Dictionary of Political Biography (Oxford: Oxford University Press, 1998), 4, https://www.questia.com/read/34683386.

Adenauer

Chapter 4: A Divided Nation

With tensions between the West and East high, Germany officially became two countries in 1949, with the West called the Federal Republic of Germany and the East the German Democratic Republic.[21] The Eastern half was closely linked to the Soviet government and rejected the existence of West Germany, claiming East Germany was "the only legal German state, to which the future of Germany belongs."[22] For his part, Ulbricht dreamed of building an East Germany that could compete with the West, instituting 5 year plans

---

[21] Ibid.
[22] Ibid. 11.

and insisting that "[t]he victory of the working people over the exploiters and slave holders is at the same time the victorious struggle for liberation by the German people".

Most historians agree that the German Democratic Republic was little more than a puppet state of the Soviet Union, especially during the early years of its existence. It is also true that the Federal Republic of Germany was not a sovereign nation until 10 years after the conclusion of the war. The allied nations, led by the Americans, negotiated with West German authorities to reinstate the sovereignty of the West Germany.

In the midst of this in 1952, Stalin came forward with a "peace note" offering to reorganize Germany and unite it as a neutral nation, but the West considered this nothing more than timely propaganda designed to cause division within West Germany about accepting the terms of the Allies for recognition of West Germany as an independent state. Stalin suggested not that the countries be united, but that West Germany gain her independence and not become a member of any western alliance. The Allies, as well as many West Germans, did not believe they could trust the Soviets to respect West Germany's neutrality and stated that the time for negotiation with Stalin had passed. American foreign policymakers such as Henry Kissinger also suggested that a neutral Germany would have to be very heavily armed in order to defend herself in the midst of Europe, especially with the Soviet satellite states all along her border. Since "a strong, unified Germany in the center of the continent pursuing purely national policy had proved incompatible with the peace of Europe[23]", this could not be an acceptable solution.

In 1952, the Inner German Border between East and West Germany was constructed by the East German government, and from then on, "the inner-German border became one of Cold War Europe's most menacing frontiers—

---

[23] Wilke, Manfred. The Path to the Berlin Wall: Critical Stages in the History of Divided Germany. New York: Berghahn Books, 2014.88.

an 858-mile death-strip of barbed wire fences, control points, watchtowers, mines, and, later, automatic shooting devices".[24] It is important to remember that while the rate of deaths for those attempting to cross the Berlin Wall between 1961 and 1989 is often estimated to be about 200, nearly another 700 East Germans were killed crossing the Inner German border during the same period.[25]

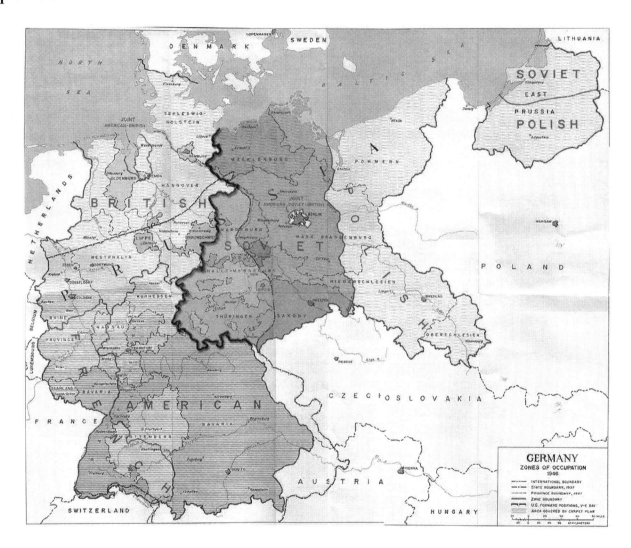

The route of the border in black

[24] David Clay Large, *Berlin* (New York: Basic Books, 2000), 425, https://www.questia.com/read/100504423.
[25] Jim Willis, *Daily Life behind the Iron Curtain* (Santa Barbara, CA: Greenwood, 2013), 113

Pictures of various sections of the Inner German border

In an attempt to control the people of East Berlin and avoid contact with Westerners, Ulbricht worked to isolate East Berliners. Berlin historian David Clay Large notes that by 1952, East Germany was already feeling the effects of failed agricultural collectivization schemes, extreme production quotas, the nationalization of major industry, and neglect of consumer goods. After the Inner German border's completion in 1952, East Germans could only leave for the west through the city of Berlin, but they continued to do so in droves, with over 130,000 leaving in just the second half of 1952 and the first 3 months of 1953. Ironically, instead of changing or moderating some of the demands the government was making on East German workers, Ulbricht upped production quotas to even higher levels.[26]

After West Germany regained sovereignty as an independent nation in

[26] David Clay Large, *Berlin* (New York: Basic Books, 2000), 425, https://www.questia.com/read/100504423.

1955, it signed the North Atlantic Treaty and became a member of NATO. NATO member nations delivered a declaration to the effect that "They consider the government of the Federal Republic as the only German government freely and legitimately constituted and therefore entitled to speak for Germany as the representative of the German people in international affairs."[27]

Meanwhile, by 1955, East Germany was attempting to combat the "brain drain" directly through propaganda messages to the East German people. According to the Eastern Bloc, those who desired to leave the communist state were being fooled by capitalist propaganda and puppets of the western fascists:

> "In both from the moral standpoint as well as in terms of the interests of the whole German nation, leaving the GDR is an act of political and moral backwardness and depravity. Those who let themselves be recruited objectively serve West German Reaction and militarism, whether they know it or not. Is it not despicable when for the sake of a few alluring job offers or other false promises about a "guaranteed future" one leaves a country in which the seed for a new and more beautiful life is sprouting, and is already showing the first fruits, for the place that favours a new war and destruction?
>
> Is it not an act of political depravity when citizens, whether young people, workers, or members of the intelligentsia, leave and betray what our people have created through common labour in our republic to offer themselves to the American or British secret services or work for the West German factory owners, Junkers, or militarists? Does not leaving the land of progress for the morass of an historically outdated social order demonstrate political

---

[27] Wilke, Manfred. The Path to the Berlin Wall: Critical Stages in the History of Divided Germany. New York: Berghahn Books, 2014.87.

backwardness and blindness? ...[W]orkers throughout Germany will demand punishment for those who today leave the German Democratic Republic, the strong bastion of the fight for peace, to serve the deadly enemy of the German people, the imperialists and militarists."[28]

An indication of just how bad conditions got is that the Soviets began to advise Ulbricht to ease off of collectivization and production quotas. The Soviets were becoming embarrassed by the mass defections to the west and feared that if protests were to arise in East Germany, they could spread to other communist regimes, or even the Soviet Union itself. However, for political reasons, Ulbricht refused; he had seen the results for others who had not followed a hard line approach in the past, and he believed the best way to save himself was to continue to demand more from the East German people. Thus, in defiance of the Soviets, he increased quotas by an additional 25 percent.

Finally, a group of construction workers began an informal strike that spread quickly and grew out of control in a matter of days. With the world watching, the Soviets knew they had to act quickly to leave no question about what would happen if communist authority were questioned. Soviet tanks rolled into East Berlin and the East German secret police were unleashed on the people. In the immediate clash, over 200 were killed, and almost 5,000 were arrested. The uprising, though embarrassing to the Soviets, likely guaranteed Ulbricht would remain in power despite his disobedience so that any appearance of "giving into protests" might be avoided.[29]

One historian sees the lack of action on the part of the various forces in Berlin as an important lesson for the USSR in the future. By not intervening in the violent response to East German protests, "what the Western Allies

---

[28] ("He Who Leaves the German Democratic Republic Joins the Warmongers", Notizbuch des Agitators ("Agitator's Notebook"), Berlin: Socialist Unity Party's Agitation Department, November 1955.
[29] Ibid. 429-430.

seemed to be saying was that the Soviets and GDR authorities had carte blanche in East Berlin, so long as they did not try to push the Western powers out of West Berlin. It was a message that the Soviets, the GDR government, and most of all the East German people, would not soon forget".[30]

Chapter 5: Khrushchev's Demands for West Berlin

For all of his prominence and power within the Soviet Union, Nikita Khrushchev was a virtual unknown in the outside world when he succeeded Stalin, and the West was less than impressed to say the least. Looking at the short, heavyset Russian who wore ill-fitting suits, Khrushchev was dismissed as a buffoon. British Foreign Secretary Harold Macmillan labeled him a "fat, vulgar man" and predicted he would not last long.

However, the "buffoon" soon showed the West he was not to be trifled with. At every turn, Khrushchev took the tactic of confrontation over conciliation. A believer in the ultimate superiority of the Soviet System, Khrushchev wanted to position the Soviet Union as a player on the world stage, an equal to the Western Allies—particularly the United States. His view was summarized in a statement made to Western diplomats at the Polish Embassy in Moscow: "We will bury you." Khrushchev didn't appear to be engaging in hyperbole either; the statement came as Soviet forces were crushing an uprising in Hungary that led to the deaths of nearly 4,000 Hungarians. That said, this confrontational persona was quite at odds with how Khrushchev would later be described by a biographer ("He could be charming or vulgar, ebullient or sullen, he was given to public displays of rage (often contrived) and to soaring hyperbole in his rhetoric. But whatever he was, however he came across, he was more human than his predecessor or even than most of his foreign counterparts, and for much of the world that was enough to make the USSR seem less mysterious or menacing.").

The timeline for the wall's construction may be said to have started on

---

[30] Ibid.

November 10, 1958. After 6 years of a divided German border, Khrushchev decided to demand that West Berlin and East Berlin be united and the city become "part of the state on whose land it is situated".[31] After floating the idea in public, Khrushchev followed up with communication to his former allies in France, London, and Washington concerning his "Natural solution", but he also suggested that if Berlin were not to become a fully East German city, another acceptable solution might be reached in making West Berlin an independent "free city" under the United Nations.[32] At this time, he also issued a 6 month timeline for the city to be returned to East Germany or given "free status". According to Khrushchev, "the German Democratic Republic had scrupulously observed the stipulations of the Potsdam Agreement with regard to the eradication of militarism and liquidation of the monopolies while the Western Powers had permitted the revival of militarism and economic imperialism in the German Federal Republic".[33]

Khrushchev stepped up the pressure, particularly in the U.S., believing that he could successfully use the prospect of war to convince the United States to give up its position in Berlin. U.S. ambassador Averill Harriman heard this from Khrushchev in the early summer of 1959: "We are determined to liquidate your rights in West Berlin. What good does it do for you to have eleven thousand troops in Berlin? If it came to war, we would swallow them in one gulp.... You can start a war if you like, but remember, it will be you who are starting it, not we.... West Germany knows that we could destroy it in ten minutes.... If you start a war, we may die, but the rockets will fly automatically."[34]

At the same time, Khrushchev also seemed to offer a greater openness to the West. For the first time, Khrushchev allowed American tourists to come into the country, and likewise, he allowed limited numbers of Soviet citizens to

---

[31] Ibid. 438.
[32] Ibid. 439.
[33] (State Department, 1962, p. 2). qtd. in CIA Report
[34] Ibid.

travel in the West. He was particularly interested in trade and cultural ties; since he believed in the inherent superiority of the communist system, he wanted the West to see Soviet achievements, and he also wanted Soviets to know their country was at least the equal to the West and would soon surpass it.

As a part of this opening to the West, Khrushchev was visited by then Vice President Richard M. Nixon in 1959. Nixon was the highest-ranking American official to visit the world's first Communist superpower, even though in those years, Nixon (who as president would spearhead a series of policies known as Détente that would ease the rhetoric of the Cold War) was known as a leading anti-communist who successfully led the charge against Alger Hiss. This visit became famous for the "Kitchen Debate;" In a model kitchen at the American National Exhibition in Moscow, Nixon and Khrushchev engaged in a spirited argument wherein each defended the other's economic system. Nixon's visit prompted an invitation to Khrushchev to visit the United States.

Nixon and Khrushchev

Khrushchev became the first Soviet leader to visit an American president since the end of World War II in September 1959. For 13 days, he toured the country, fueling a media frenzy. Landing at Washington D.C. with his wife Nina Petrovna and his adult children, he proceeded to visit New York City, Los Angeles, San Francisco, Iowa, Pittsburgh, and Washington. Unfortunately for the premier, a visit to Disneyland had to be cancelled for security reasons. The trip ended with a meeting with President Eisenhower at Camp David, where the two leaders agreed to hold a summit on Berlin to settle the issues on the city. Khrushchev left the U.S. considering his visit a success, believing he had developed a strong relationship with Eisenhower, who did not feel the same way. Regardless, the president was scheduled to visit Moscow in 1960.

It was a visit that was to not to take place. On May 1, 1960 Soviet surface-to-air missiles shot down a U-2 spy plane piloted by Francis Gary Powers. The flights, which had long angered the Soviets, had been resumed after a long halt. Khrushchev held off announcing the shoot down until May 5, worried that the incident would jeopardize the summit scheduled for May 15. When the announcement was made, Khrushchev tried to blame the flights on rogue elements in the American military, trying to deflect possible blame from Eisenhower. The president, however, admitted that the flights had occurred and that he had ordered them, which put Khrushchev in a very difficult position with the summit approaching.

The Paris Summit was disaster for Khrushchev. When he arrived, he demanded an apology from Eisenhower and a promise of no more U-2 over flights. He got no apology, but Eisenhower had already suspended the flights and offered his Open Skies proposal for mutual overflight rights. Khrushchev refused, and left the summit, and Eisenhower's visit to the Soviet Union was cancelled.

The collapse of the Paris Summit ended Khrushchev's "soft approach" to the West. In his September 1960 visit to the U.N. General Assembly, he showed his "hard approach". Rather than trying to charm the West, he began the Soviet Union's wooing of the new Third-World countries in an effort to bring them into the Soviet orbit. Of course, that effort was largely forgotten by Khrushchev's personal histrionics. During a speech by a Filipino delegate criticizing the Soviet Union for decrying colonialism while engaging in it, he took off his shoe and began banging it repeatedly on his table while calling the speaker a "jerk, stooge, and lackey", and "a toady of American imperialism". When the Romanian Foreign Vice-Minister began vocally attacking the Filipino delegate, his microphone was cut off, leading to jeers among Eastern bloc members. his microphone was eventually shut off, prompting a chorus of shouts and jeers from the Eastern Bloc delegations. The meeting was immediately adjourned, with Assembly President Frederick Boland slamming his gavel down so hard that the head broke off and went flying.

Khrushchev at the United Nations in September 1960

Meanwhile, as Eisenhower's second term was coming to an end in 1960, the administration readied a military defense plan for West Berlin, even though they were loathe to put it into action and hoped that the Soviets would not take any action that would force a response. The plan included the use of nuclear warheads, and it was communicated to West German leader Adenauer that 1.5 million German casualties could be expected if it had to be put into effect.[35]

---

[35] Ibid, 440.

Why would the United States even consider such a response? Berlin had little strategic value to its former allies (though some spy operations had been being conducted out of and even under the city since 1945), and the city was not even particularly popular with Germans themselves. The United States had to realize that a war with the Soviets over West Berlin would be devastating and would cost lives on both sides.

The other option, however, was the one that proved to be unthinkable. In the years since the division of the city, West Berlin had become a symbol of hope against communist oppression and against the Soviet domination of Europe. The Berlin Airlift had dominated the news and been reported around the world. To allow the communists to take West Berlin without a military protest would be to give silent approval to Soviet aggression and send a message to Khrushchev that his actions would be tolerated if the threat level was high enough. This could destabilize the rest of Europe as well, and the Allies had been down the road of appeasement all too recently. Eisenhower determined that he would "rather be atomized than communized".[36]

In an interesting look backward, Khrushchev's son gave a 2009 interview regarding his father's trip to America and had this to say when asked about the topic of whether or not the Berlin ultimatum was genuine: "I think it was not a bluff because it was an abnormal situation because it was two powers, or super powers, the United States and the Soviet Union. And they met, or maybe they confronted on the problem: recognition of East Berlin, or rather East Germany. For the Soviet Union, East Germany was part of the Soviet Bloc, and it was an independent country. For the United States, and the Western part of the world it was the zone of the Soviet Occupation, and it was only one Germany: West Germany. My Father tried to do everything to push Western countries for the recognition of East Germany, and he did everything. Because it was endless negotiations before that, he imposed this ultimatum that maybe he thought he would be able to declare that in the

---

36 Ibid. 430-441.

beginning he thought that now if we recognize East Germany, then the West will recognize it, or some similar rationale. But facing the strong opposition of the West, he changed his mind, and decided that it would be too high a price to bring the confrontation to such a level, and so it was better to try to bring Americans - because it was mostly an American position, the Europeans were ready to recognize East Germany de facto - to bring them to negotiations so I would not say that it is right to call it a bluff."[37]

David Large offers an assessment heard commonly amongst historians regarding the Khrushchev trip in that it made "no progress".

Chapter 6: Khrushchev and Kennedy

After the disaster of the Paris Summit and his performance at the U.N. General Assembly, Khrushchev hoped for a new beginning with the United States with the election of John F. Kennedy as the new U.S. President. Khrushchev saw Kennedy as a more likely partner in achieving an easing of tensions than the defeated Nixon; but once again, Khrushchev misjudged yet another American President. What Khrushchev did not know (or if he knew, ignored) was that the new President was himself an anti-communist who had little interest in "détente" with the Soviet Union. Kennedy's first few months in office were marked by tough talk.

Within just a month of becoming President, the issue of communist Cuba became central to the Kennedy Presidency. On February 3rd, 1961, President Kennedy called for a plan to support Cuban refugees in the U.S. A month later, Kennedy created the Peace Corps, a program that trained young American volunteers to help with economic and community development in poor countries. Both programs were integral pieces of the Cold War: each was an attempt to align disadvantaged groups abroad with the United State and the West, against the Soviet Union and its Communist satellites.

[37] Kyle Kordon Interview with Sergei Khrushchev 2009 GET INFO

Cuba and the Cold War boiled over in April, when the Kennedy Administration moved beyond soft measures to direct action. From April 17-20, 1,400 CIA-trained Cuban exiles landed on the beaches of Western Cuba in an attempt to overthrow Fidel Castro. This plan, which Kennedy called the "Bay of Pigs," had been originally drafted by the Eisenhower Administration. The exiles landed in Cuba and were expected to be greeted by anti-Castro forces within the country. After this, the US was to provide air reinforcement to the rebels, and the Castro regime would slowly be overthrown.

By April 19th, however, it became increasingly clear to Kennedy that the invasion would not work. The exiles were not, as expected, greeted by anti-Castro forces. Instead, the Cuban government captured or killed all of the invaders. No U.S. air reinforcement was ever provided, flummoxing both the exiles and American military commanders. The Bay of Pigs had been an unmitigated disaster.

Unfortunately for the young president, April 1961 also witnessed the first manned space flight by Soviet cosmonaut Yuri Gagarin, handing the Soviets two propaganda victories. But the embarrassment of the failure in Cuba stiffened Kennedy's resolve not to make any concessions to the Soviets at the Vienna Summit on June 3, 1961. In their first and only face-to-face meeting (and the last meeting between a Soviet Leader and an American president until Nixon), neither man was in a mood to compromise. Khrushchev renewed his demands, but he also demanded that the U.S. withdraw all troops from West Berlin, allowing it to unite with East Berlin under GDR control. As a halfway measure, Khrushchev said he would accept Berlin as a free city without ties to the West. The leaders were also at loggerheads over an atmospheric test-ban treaty.

Khrushchev and Kennedy meet at Vienna

W.R. Smyser, author of *Kennedy and the Berlin Wall* argues that Kennedy was naive about Khrushchev's level of seriousness over the Berlin issue going into the Vienna summit because his ambassadors had not correctly communicated Khrushchev's anger and urgency on the matter. Khrushchev had told the Czechs that he planned to scare Kennedy into doing what he wanted in Berlin. He also believed humiliating Kennedy in Berlin would accomplish his further goals of causing NATO members to lose faith in the promises of the American government and scaring away Western investors from West Germany, thus leaving the country open to a takeover.[38]

During the meeting, Khrushchev alternated between calm and, as Kennedy later described it, "going berserk". He claimed that the United States was asking the Soviet Union "to sit like schoolboy with his hands on his desk" and that since the Soviet Union believed so strongly in the ideas of communism "it [could not] guarantee that these ideas will stop at its borders".[39] Kennedy responded by explaining to Khrushchev the nature of his position on Berlin: "This matter is of the greatest concern to the U.S. We

[38] Smyser, W.R. Kennedy and the Berlin Wall. Rowman & Littlefield Publishers. 16 Sept. 2009. 59-60.
[39] Ibid. 66.

are in Berlin not because of someone's sufferance. We fought our way here, although our causalities may not have been as high as the U.S.S.R.'s. We are in Berlin not by agreement by East Germans, but by our contractual rights."[40]

Khrushchev did not react well to Kennedy's replies, alternately threatening and lecturing Kennedy that his position would lead to inevitable war between the two sides, and Smyser's discussion of Kennedy and Khrushchev suggests that Khrushchev's intimidation tactics may have worked to an extent: "Khrushchev may well have put in a show, deliberately throwing the kind of tantrums that he had thrown in some of his private meetings with MacMillan [the British Prime Minister]…An American journalist told a U.S. official that…Kennedy looked 'green' at the end of the summit. Another American wrote that Kennedy appeared 'dazed' by the 'sheer animal energy' of Khrushchev's presentation".[41]

Kennedy's performance in Vienna has met with mixed reactions. Some have put the blame for the construction of the Berlin Wall on what they see as Kennedy's weakness in his initial meeting with the Soviet premier, while others believe he more than adequately defended American sovereignty in a nearly impossible situation. At a 2011 CIA conference discussing the wall, the conference concluded that "Kennedy undercut his own bargaining position with the Soviet Premier when [he] conveyed US acquiescence to the permanent division of Berlin. This misstep in the negotiations made Kennedy's later, more assertive public statements, less credible to the Soviets, who now saw him as indecisive and weak".[42]

In a similar vein, Large discusses Kennedy's own frustration with the need to defend Berlin, indicating that Kennedy was not as committed to the city as he might have seemed in Vienna. Large recalls Kennedy's words to an aide: "We're stuck in a ridiculous position. It seems silly for us to be facing an

---

[40] Large 442.
[41] Smyser, 72.
[42] Carmichael.

atomic war over a treaty preserving Berlin as the future capital of a reunited Germany when all of us know that Germany will probably never be reunited".[43] Kennedy was resolute on the point that he would not use nuclear weapons to solve the Berlin crisis or defend the city. He even indicated some understanding of Khrushchev's frustration with the large amount of East Germans leaving the country through West Berlin, and he felt that the West Germans were using the Americans for defense while they rebuilt their economy. As Kennedy expressed it, "if [the West Germans] think we are rushing into a war over Berlin, except as a last desperate move to save the NATO alliance, they've got another thing coming."[44]

Willy Brandt, the mayor of Berlin, wrote in his memoir, *My Road to Berlin*, of living as a free Berliner but with his fate being controlled largely by the decisions of the superpowers: "[T]he Allied headquarters for the present still gave the impression that the West was willing to compromise the differences by making large concessions to the Russians. Time and again the representatives of America, England, and France allowed themselves to be outmaneuvered by the Soviet side. It was the time that a spokesman of Berlin expressed the mood of many of his fellow citizens in these words: 'The worst is not that we have to fight with our backs to the wall --but that the Western powers are no wall to lean against.'"[45]

Both men left the summit empty handed, and Kennedy later told his brother Bobby that it was "like dealing with Dad. All give and no take." However, Khrushchev came away from the meeting still thinking he could push the young president around, even as the failure once again to settle the question of Berlin put the Soviet premier in a difficult situation. Though the leaders of the British, French, and American governments were convinced that the Soviets would not risk an all-out-war, Khrushchev continued to threaten that if the West did not acquiesce to his demands, the Soviets would work toward

---

[43] Ibid., 443.

[44] Ibid.

[45] Willy Brandt, My Road to Berlin (Garden City, NY: Doubleday, 1960), 176, https://www.questia.com/read/55091042.

a separate peace treaty with East Germany.[46]

On June 15, 1961, Walter Ulbricht issued the following denial when asked a question in regards to a plan to separate the city: "I understand by your question that there are men in West Germany who wish that we [would] mobilize the construction workers of the GDR in order to build a wall. I don't know of any such intention. The construction workers of our country are principally occupied with home building and their strength is completely consumed by this task. Nobody has the intention of building a wall."[47] Lawrence Freedman, author of *Kennedy's Wars: Berlin, Cuba, Laos, and Vietnam*, argues that as East Germany continued to prove unable to stem the tide of East Germans leaving the country through Berlin, Ulbricht attempted to "force Khrushchev's hand" by purposely dropping (and simultaneously denying) the idea of a wall or boundary being constructed in the midst of the city.[48] Other historians claim that Ulbricht had been in negotiations with Khrushchev, who was pushing for the wall and that Ulbricht's mention of it was a slip of the tongue.

Did East German leader Walter Ulbricht come to believe that the only way to avoid East Germany's demise was to construct the wall and thus seek Soviet permission to do so, or was the wall built at the behest of Nikita Khrushchev himself, anxious to press his advantage at a time when he believed the world response would be weak enough to allow him to carry out his plan without military repercussions? The answers almost surely lie in a meeting between Khrushchev and Ulbricht that took place on August 1, 1961. In a document discovered by German historian Matthias Uhl, it appears that the main impetus came from Khrushchev; the document reveals that Khrushchev had earlier broached the subject with Ulbricht through his ambassador to Berlin, sending him to "explain to him my idea of taking

---

[46] Carmichael.

[47] Lawrence Freedman, Kennedy's Wars: Berlin, Cuba, Laos, and Vietnam (New York: Oxford University Press, 2000), 72, https://www.questia.com/read/90323460.

[48] Ibid.

advantage of the current tensions with the West and laying an iron ring around Berlin". The flow of engineers out of East Germany "had to stop," Khrushchev explained.

In the written recording of the conversation between the two leaders, Khrushchev was the clear decision-maker, with Ulbricht's willing acquiescence. It was clear that Khrushchev was disappointed in Ulbricht's performance: "When I attended your party convention two years ago, everything was fine. What happened? You wanted to pull ahead of West Germany by 1961/62…We will give you one or two weeks to make the necessary economic preparations. Then you will convene the parliament and issue the following communiqué: 'Beginning tomorrow, checkpoints will be erected and transit will be prohibited. Anyone who wishes to cross the border can do so only with the permission of certain authorities of the German Democratic Republic.'"[49] When Ulbricht made clear to Khrushchev his desire to include his economic ministers in on the decision for the wall, Khrushchev refused, saying, "You should not explain anything before the introduction of the new border regime. It would only strengthen the flow of people leaving." If word got out about the wall construction, the Kremlin director recognized correctly, there could be "traffic jams" on Berlin's access roads. Such forms of traffic obstruction would constitute "a certain demonstration," he said.

Whatever the case, the wall's construction would begin about two months later.

Chapter 7: The Wall's Construction

In the midst of negotiations, summits, and threats, East Germans continued to leave the country via Berlin at unprecedented rates. June 1961 saw approximately 19,000 leave, and July brought the exodus of another 30,000.

---

[49] Wiegrefe, Klaus. "The Khrushchev Connection: Who Ordered the Construction of the Berlin Wall?". Speigel Online International. August 23, 2009.

By the 11th of August, another 16,000 were gone, and on August 12 alone, 2,400 East Germans exited the country in what would be the only legal way to do so for the next 28 years.[50] The East German parliament issued the following proclamation on August 11th, 1961: "The People's Assembly confirms the impending measures to protect the security of the GDR and to curtail the campaign of organized Kopfjägerei [head-hunting] and Menschenhandel [traffic in human lives] orchestrated from West Germany and West Berlin. The Assembly empowers the GDR Council of Ministers to undertake all the steps approved by the member states of the Warsaw Pact. The Assembly appeals to all peace-loving citizens of the GDR to give their full support to the agencies of their Workers-and-Peasants State in the application of these measures."[51]

Few would have predicted that the "impending measures" would produce the wall that would divide Berlin and the world for almost three decades, but on Sunday, August 13, East German soldiers began to install posts and connect barbed wire to seal off the eastern part of the city.

[50] "Berlin Wall". *History.com* 2009. Web. February 11, 2015.
[51] Ibid. 446.

East Germans sealing the border and installing barbed wire on August 13

What caused the wall to be built on the 13th rather than another day? Permission for the barbed wire portion of the wall had been granted on August 5th, and Large argues that several signs from the Americans gave Khrushchev the impression that the United States would not take action if the wall was constructed. The remarks of American Senator William Fulbright were also seen by many as an encouragement to Khrushchev. On an ABC news show on July 30th, 1961, Fulbright discussed the heavy losses of man and brainpower being experienced by East Germany and remarked, "I don't understand why the East Germans don't close their border, because I think they have a right to close it."[52]

In fact, Khrushchev himself gave direct orders to the East Germans constructing the wall that the initial attempt at a barrier be made only with wire and fence posts to test the West's response. When none was

[52] Jack Kenny, "The Wall, Hiding Shame: The Berlin Wall Was Erected in 1961 to Stop the Continual Flight of East Germans to the West, Owing to the Abject Failure of Collectivism in the Soviet-Bloc Country," The New American, August 22, 2011, https://www.questia.com/read/1G1-265977875.

forthcoming, he gave the go-ahead for concrete block walls to be put into place beginning on the 15th of August.

The construction of the wall on August 15

All told, the wall itself was constructed by 32,000 East German engineers with materials that had been collected over a multiple months in preparation for the divide.[53] In an article in *Antiquity*, Frederick Baker seeks to change misconceptions about the wall that he believes exist because of the tourism generated by pieces of the wall after 1989. Baker explains, "'The Wall' was a set of in-depth border fortifications that consisted of two parallel walls: an interior and an exterior one enclosed a 'death strip' and watch-towers".[54] The interior wall was more of a makeshift border control that involved the use of barbed wire, abandoned buildings, and even small bodies of water.

Baker also set forth the four phases of construction of the wall that separated East and West Berliners from each other for 28 years. The first

---

[53] John S. Brown, "The Erstwhile Berlin Wall at 50," Army, August 2011, https://www.questia.com/read/1P3-2413938141.

[54] Frederick Baker, "The Berlin Wall: Production, Preservation and Consumption of a 20th-Century Monument," Antiquity 67, no. 257 (1993), https://www.questia.com/read/1G1-15143722.

phase of the wall was initially constructed of wire, fence posts, and chipped cobblestone from the surrounding streets and the surrounding of the city was complete by the afternoon of August 14th. Reinforced sections of concrete were added to this when the Soviets become assured that the West would not attempt to remove the original wire barriers. Though Baker describes the first phase of the wall as "flimsy", he admits that it was largely effective at stemming the tide of East Germans leaving the country.[55]

There were issues with the wall, especially along the Bernauer Strasse, where occupied residences actually made up part of the construction and people could walk or jump their way to the west. Furthermore, underground trains could still travel underneath the wall, as long as no stops were made in East Berlin. After the East Germans determined that the potential (and actual) escapes were too great of a risk, they bulldozed the homes along the Bernauer Strasse, built an exterior wall on the other side of it, and created what would become known as the "death strip".[56]

[55] Ibid.
[56] Mark Ehrman, "Borders and Barriers," The Virginia Quarterly Review 83, no. 2 (2007), https://www.questia.com/read/1P3-1256577881.

Pictures of the death strip

The second phase of the wall was all concrete, with smooth pipe at the top in most sections. This wall was more permanent and impressive, as well as more secure since it included 260 guard towers. This section included embedded flares ready to go off, trip wires lying under the sand that surrounded the guard tower road, dogs ready to chase down and attack potential escapees, and 5 inch spikes designed to impale the feet or bodies of any who attempted to jump from the top of the wall. The division of the city was so important to the East that even the sewage system that lay underneath the city was secured.[57]

---

[57] Baker.

In 1976, a third version of the wall was begun, and this is the one that most people remember since it was in existence when the wall came down in 1989. Though under public pressure, some of the more flagrant "defenses" were no longer a part, but it's important not to discount the huge psychological effect the massive final version of the wall had on those contemplating the "crime" of leaving East Germany: "The symbolic discouragement should not be exaggerated in comparison with the physical: the order to shoot, in operation on the border since the 1950s, became a part of the official constitution in May 1982".[58]

In conjunction with the Berlin Wall was the Inner German Wall, stretching over 870 miles, dividing East Germany from West Germany, and guarded on the eastern side by frontier troops known as *Grentztruppen*.[59]

[58] Ibid.
[59] Rottman, Gordon. The Berlin Wall and the Inner German Border 1961-1989, New York: Osprey Publishing, 2008,4.

Chapter 8: Reaction to the Wall's Construction

Many observers of the days and nights following August 13th would be witness to divided couples, friends, and business partners separated by the wall that seemed to appear out of nowhere. Norman Gelb, who was the Mutual Broadcasting System correspondent in Berlin at the time of the building of the wall, was allowed to enter East Germany during the immediate days after August 13th when the Soviets were still allowing foreign nationals to cross the border between East and West Berlin somewhat freely. He recalls one of the most poignant scenes being East Germans who had packed their things and made it to the border between the cities, only to find that they had been sealed into East Germany. Compounding that misfortune was the fact that as they made their way back to their homes, they knew they had exposed themselves to the East German Secret Police.[60]

The construction of the wall not only separated families and friends but also instilled fear among the German leadership in the west. Some of the concern was based on the hope that West Berliners would not partake in any violence against the soldiers and party members constructing the wall, which might provide an excuse for an East German or Soviet attack on West Berlin itself. Kennedy, however, did not fear such an attack. As he saw it, "Why would Khrushchev put up a wall if he really intended to seize West Berlin? There shouldn't be any need of a wall if he occupied the whole city. This is his way out of his predicament. It's not a nice solution, but a wall is a hell of a lot better than a war".[61]

Of course, not everyone, least of all West Berliners, appreciated Kennedy's take on the new wall that divided their city. As the wall was going up, Brandt complained, "The Berlin Senate publicly condemns the illegal and inhuman measures being taken by those who are dividing Germany. The cold concrete

---

[60] Norman Gelb, "The Wall That Shut out the West," The Christian Science Monitor, August 14, 1996, https://www.questia.com/read/1P2-33414015.

[61] Ibid., 452.

stakes that cut through our city have been driven into the heart of German unity and into the living organism of our single city of Berlin". Three days later, Brandt heavily criticized Kennedy in writing for his lack of response, saying of the wall's ongoing construction, "I think this is a serious turning point in the post-war history of the city as it has not been seen since the blockade. The development has not changed the resistance or will of the people of West Berlin, but it was likely to raise doubts in the reaction ability and determination of the three powers… Inactivity and pure defensiveness could cause a crisis of confidence with the Western powers. I consider the situation serious enough, Mr. President, to write to you in all frankness as is possible only between friends who trust each other completely…"[62]

   Kennedy was angered by Brandt's letter, but he did send Vice President Lyndon Johnson and General Lucius Clay (who had orchestrated the Berlin Airlift) to help reassure Berliners that the United States had not abandoned them. On August 19th, Johnson delivered a speech to the welcoming crowds that had gathered in West Berlin, promising, "To the survival and to the creative future of this city we Americans have pledged, in effect, what our ancestors pledged in forming the United States—'our lives, our fortunes, and our sacred honor.' The President wants you to know and I want you to know that the pledge he has given to the freedom of West Berlin and to the rights of Western access to Berlin is firm…. This island does not stand alone."[63]

   Some Germans believed that the United States had failed to protect Germany, claiming that they could and should have prevented the building of the wall in the months leading up to August 13th. Those who hold to this position would argue that since the West had initially acted as administrators in the division of Berlin and Germany, had put such severe limitations on the military development of West Germany, and entered into NATO alliance with it, the building of the wall can be laid at the feat of a United States for

---

[62] "Brief des Regierenden Bürgermeisters von Berlin, Willy Brandt, an den amerikanischen Präsidenten John F. Kennedy" 16. August 1961. *Chronik der Mauer*. Translated from the German.
[63] Large, 455.

acting ambiguously instead of directly.[64]

However, in her 1967 book *The Wall is Not Forever*, Eleanor Dulles explains that while the nine weeks that followed Kennedy and Khrushchev's meetings were characterized with concern over the next move of the Soviets, the idea of an actual wall of separation being constructed was not taken seriously. Despite the flurry of speculation about the fallout of Kennedy and Khrushchev's discussion, German newspapers were not speculating on a physical division of the city. Dulles quotes one German as remembering, "In no West Berlin newspaper was the possibility of a total control and eventual [counter] measures seriously discussed.... No one believed that the regime would go as far as to take the measures for a complete sealing off."[65] It was, however, the general opinion in East Germany that American equivocation on their position on Berlin meant that East Germans who wanted to leave their country before it was too late needed to do so immediately. This led to an increase in emigrations that threatened the viability of East German factories, agriculture, and even the survival of the East German state.[66]

Once the wall was constructed, anger was unleashed at both the Soviets and the Americans. In remembrance of Neville Chamberlain's appeasement of the Nazis in Munich in the years leading to World War II, Berlin schoolchildren sent John F. Kennedy a black umbrella.[67] This was ironic since Khrushchev tried to distance himself from the wall to an extent, even as he did not want to lose the impression that he was taking a hard line against the West. In a conversation with the ambassador to West Germany, he explained, "I wouldn't want to conceal from you that it was I who in the last instance gave the order for it...I know that the Wall is an ugly thing. It will also disappear. However only when the reasons for its construction have gone".[68]

---

[64] Eleanor Lansing Dulles, *Berlin: The Wall Is Not Forever* (Chapel Hill, NC: University of North Carolina Press, 1967), 49,
    https://www.questia.com/read/30327334.
[65] Ibid.
[66] Ibid. 51.
[67] Large, 452.

Though Khrushchev was interested in Berlin in the long term, the mass exodus of young people from a country already faced with production and technological deficits was the immediate concern of the Soviet premier: "What was I supposed to do? More than 30,000 people, the best and most capable of the country, left the GDR in July. It is quite easy to calculate the moment of breakdown of the East German economy if we had not done something to stop the mass flight. There were only two alternatives: an air transport blockade, or the Wall. The former would have caused trouble with the USA which might have led to war. I could not and did not want to risk this. Therefore, the Wall was the only solution."[69]

Public relations were, ironically, very important to Soviet-controlled East Germany in the years that followed the creation of the wall (when the largest amount of escape attempts were made). The Soviets were aware that walling off of a city could not look positive to the parts of the world in which they did not control the press, but they insisted on "anti-fascist rampart" rhetoric despite this fact. When people attempting to cross the border were killed, therefore, the "corpse cases" that resulted were to be handled by the Stasi, the East German secret police. Bodies were transported to medical facilities or universities for autopsy and study. Those injured in an attack were transported by army vehicles rather than ambulances, and they were sent to hospitals further away for the prying eyes of the press rather than to the closest hospitals where a person might get the best or most immediate care.[70]

Of course, those outside of the Eastern Bloc things saw things far differently. Shortly before the fall of the Berlin wall in 1989, an American named Gerald Kelinfeld spoke in West Berlin about what the wall symbolized to Americans: "For the Americans, the wall is a symbol of injustice, of inhumanity, of disrespect for human rights; perhaps it is more important than for some West Germans and West Berliners…The United

---

[68] Ruhle & Holzwei qtd. in Baker.
[69] Mark Ehrman, "Borders and Barriers," The Virginia Quarterly Review 83, no. 2 (2007), https://www.questia.com/read/1P3-1256577881.
[70] Ibid.

States is here because of national interests, but also because of political ideals. This is precisely the point. Every American administration advocates the right of the German people to self-determination. Public support is broad and deep. When the wall turned twenty-five, even provincial newspapers in the United States contained comprehensive coverage of the history and significance of this monument."[71]

At the time of the wall's construction, however, the West was taken somewhat by surprise. In retrospect, some have asked if the United States should have committed troops to Berlin to stop the construction of the massive wall that divided families for 28 years. These wonder if, at the point of the wall's origin, when it was still more of a threat than a reality, its permanency could have been avoided: "The frail strands of wire and wooden booms manned by soldiers in August 13 and 14, with only a few cement and stone obstructions, could have been breached. There were even a few crossing points open, but the separation probably could not have been thwarted except in terms of a major contest between the United States and the USSR."

Either way, it's clear that the United States was not ready to take on that major contest in 1961. On August 13th, Secretary of State Dean Rusk informed John F. Kennedy that the wall was being built, yet Kennedy continued with his plans to go sailing in Hyannis Port.[72] That makes clear that the administration was not even considering military action against the East Germans or Soviets, although they would condemn the action. As Khrushchev had predicted in 1959, "The leaders of the United States are not such idiots as to fight over Berlin."[73]

Moreover, the leaders of France and Britain, Charles DeGaulle and Harold McMillan, showed even less concern over the initial construction of the wall.

---

[71] Wilke, Manfred. The Path to the Berlin Wall: Critical Stages in the History of Divided Germany. New York: Berghahn Books, 2014.

[72] Yosefa Loshitzky, "Constructing and Deconstructing the Wall," *CLIO* 26, no. 3 (1997), https://www.questia.com/read/1G1-19984489.

[73] David Clay Large, *Berlin* (New York: Basic Books, 2000), https://www.questia.com/read/100504423.

Neither leader immediately returned to their capital to address the situation. Both countries had their militaries and budgets committed to other places in the world, and neither believed that the people they had worked so hard to defeat only 15 years ago were worth defending to the death simply because their city was divided.[74]

The successful construction of the wall surprised not only the West but the East as well. Since the East Germans and Soviets were fully aware that the West had several options to stop construction, in the initial stages simply by removing physical barriers, making use of the uniformed reserve troops that Kennedy ordered to Berlin in the aftermath, or even by the use of nuclear weapons against the East Germans, they were emboldened when they found there would be little response. Thus, in the months that followed construction of the initial wall and border, harassment of allied officials crossing into East Berlin began to become regular. At checkpoints Alpha and Bravo, guards began interfering in the "unhindered access" of Western officials into East Berlin, which was a clear violation of the 1945 agreements between the powers.

The occupying force that remained in Western Europe came from Britain, France, and the United States. One young boy, the son of a British RAF officer, grew up in West Germany and recalled occasional trips to "gray" East Berlin with the family. His mother recorded her thoughts on one such visit: "Our visit to East Berlin was memorable. We arrived in our car at Checkpoint Charlie (the only place allied troops could cross over). It was all rather chaotic with many vehicles vying for space, overseen by watchtowers and one small guard hut. Your dad had to wear RAF No. 1 dress uniform to enter East Berlin. We wondered how long we would need to queue when a guard noticed your dad and we got pulled to the front of the queue and through the barrier and into East Berlin. The contrast to the West was

---

[74] "The Berlin Wall: A Secret History: The Berlin Wall Was a Tangible Symbol of the Suppression of Human Rights by the Eastern Bloc during the Cold War, but Frederick Taylor Asks Whether It Was More Convenient to the Western Democracies Than Their Rhetoric Suggested," History Today, February 2007, https://www.questia.com/read/1G1-159921707.

striking. There were hardly any people walking around. Almost no cars on the streets, certainly none like our VW cabriolet. We drove around, stopping to look at various sites. You dad was convinced we were followed everywhere. We were only allowed into certain shops, and not many at that. The shops mainly sold gifts; chessboards with hand carved pieces, Russian dolls, that sort of thing. People weren't generally talkative, but someone said that most of the 'gifts' were made by Russian prisoners in the gulags."

It is Checkpoint Charlie, however, that's name has become synonymous with the confrontation that took place at the wall in the midst of the Cold War. On October 22, 1961, a senior U.S. diplomat on the way to an opera house in East Berlin was asked for his passport by the East German border guards at Checkpoint Charlie. The diplomat protested that by the rules of the 1945 agreement between the Allies, only Soviets, not East Germans, had the right to do so, but he was denied access. General Clay responded to the incident by sending American diplomats across the border with military escorts, practically daring the East to stop the American military police. By October 27th, 1961, Clay ordered 10 U.S. tanks to the checkpoint area, and they lined up in formation facing East Berlin across the Freidrichstrasse. 10 Soviet tanks soon appeared on the other side of the checkpoint, ordered there by Moscow.[75] With armed and ready American and Soviet tanks now facing off less than 500 feet away from each other, the situation had truly reached a crisis point. After a 17 hour standoff of Russian and American tanks, the Russians stood down, removing one tank as a result of a call Kennedy placed to Khrushchev's government.[76] The immediate crisis ended as the U.S. followed suit, and one by one the tanks left the area.

[75] Colitt, Leslie."Berlin Crisis: The Standoff at Checkpoint Charlie". The Guardian. 24 October 2011. Web. 16 February 2015.
[76] Large, 456.

Checkpoint Charlie in 1963 from the West's side

Clay

Chapter 9: Escaping

In 2011, the Cold War International History Project issued a report after investigating the circumstances of almost 600 deaths at, near, or involving the Berlin Wall to provide and accurate accounting of the number of deaths caused by "either an attempted escape or a temporal and spatial link between the death and the border regime".[77] The report features explanations of how many of those who tried to cross either the wall or the Inner German border died, as well as how their deaths were handled by the East Germans. In addition to that, in only a few months, the East German government had over

---

[77] Hertle, Hans-Hermann and Maria Nooke. "The Victims at the Berlin Wall, 1961-1989". *Cold War International History Project.* August 2011.

10,000 political prisoners, which were very expensive to keep in confinement. It was at this time that the East German government contacted their counterparts about the possibility of West Germany purchasing political prisoners. The rationale provided was that the East was losing their education investment with every young person that left the GDR, and over the years of the wall's existence, West German did negotiate the purchase of release for many who were captured attempting to flee the East.[78]

It is difficult to make generalizations about those who escaped East Germany between 1961 and 1989. This group would include the young and old, males and females, and everyday citizens as well as soldiers and officials. In attempting to find some commonalities among the little over 40,000 who escaped East Germany, one can point to youth, those who were separated from relatives or spouses in the West, those who desired freedom for their children, and people angry at the surveillance state that the Stasi had created in East Germany.

Almost half of the 40,000 made their escape in the first four years of the wall's existence,[79] a time when East Germans were still experiencing the shock and desperation of separation and the chances of successful escape were higher. As the information the Stasi collected on escapees grew, they adjusted security measures accordingly.

Measures of escape went from the imaginative, such as using hot air balloons, a homemade plane constructed from the parts of a Trabant automobile, an armor-plated car, or a crossing by wires, to the more conventional methods of simply walking across the border through one of the checkpoints with falsified documents. Of course, in any type of escape, the event was never mundane; all escapees risked their lives and at times, the lives or safety of anyone the Stasi discovered was a part of the plan to escape. After an East German ferry boat was "hijacked" by a few Berliners and

---

[78] Large, 459.
[79] Willis, 114-115.

successfully made it to a drop off point in West Berlin, East German passenger ships had their steering wheels removed each night and demoted its former captain to a freight worker.[80]

Some 13 tunnels were created underneath the city of Berlin, connecting escapees to freedom, but not without danger of cave-ins or being discovered. One of the most successful tunnels was dug by a group of students who had escaped to West Berlin, and this tunnel was responsible for the successful escape of 57 East Germans before its existence was betrayed to a member of the Stasi. It is interesting to note how many escape stories end in this note, but whatever the reasons, the Stasi were quite successful in rooting out plans to escape and at following leads provided by those who had been left behind. They were perhaps most successful at infiltrating groups or organizations where escape might be a topic of discussion.

All the while, the East Germans and Soviets knew the wall was a public relations problem for communism in East Germany. To combat this, they (rather unconvincingly) cast the wall in a defensive light, claiming it was the country's way of defending itself against the plotting Westerners. By 1963, security measures were getting more stringent in an attempt to stave off both escapes and the news about them which intrigued the entire world. An East German newspaper defended the measures this way: "Each shot fired from the machine gun of one of our border guards saves the lives of thousands of GDR citizens and secures millions of marks of national assets. Showing mercy to traitors means being inhumane to the entire people".[81]

While stories of people willing to risk their lives for freedom inspired the world each time news was reported of a German couple reunited, a mother sacrificing to get her child to a life of freedom, or a group of young students determined to make it across the border to freedom, stories of failed escape attempts sobered the world and drove home the harsh consequences for those

---

[80] Wilis, 118.
[81] Ibid. 122.

who sought relief from East German communism. The name Conrad Schumann became known across the globe on August 15, 1961, the very day that the more permanent features of the wall were being added. The incident took place about 4 miles north of Checkpoint Charlie. East German border guards with orders to shoot to kill anyone attempting to cross the wall, which at this time was still largely makeshift, were local Berliners who were somewhat more likely to try to escape themselves or to allow others to do so than to shoot their own fellow city-dwellers. Thus, the East German government began moving in troops from the provinces.

Conrad Schumann had volunteered for guard duty in Berlin, but he had no idea of what he would face. Both West and East Berliners taunted the soldiers for their unpopular role, with West Berliners goading them to "come over". Schumann counted the cost of leaving his family in the East, but when a running car pulled up on the West German side of the border beckoning him with an open rear door, he began running and jumped the fence, having spaced out his fellow border guards away from the spot he was guarding. An amateur photographer (who had had practice shooting horses in mid-leap) captured Schumann jumping the barbed wire in an image that would become synonymous with the hope for freedom around the world.[82]

One of the wall's most memorable stories is that of Peter Fechter, who was killed in an escape attempt on August, 17th 1962. Fechter was an 18 year old bricklayer with an impeccable work reputation, and while at work on that day, he and a colleague with whom he had previously discussed a desire to escape East Germany found an abandoned apartment with access to the border. Interested in checking out its possibilities for a possible escape route, Fechter and his co-worker removed their shoes and moved through the apartment to the rear side, where they discovered a window that had not been barricaded. Upon hearing voices, the men jumped through the window and

---

[82] Wise, James E., and Scott Baron. Dangerous Games: Faces, Incidents, and Casualties of the Cold War. Annapolis, Md.: Naval Institute Press, 2010.

began running toward the wall. Fechter, who was shot at 35 times, was hit as soon as he reached the wall, but border guards continued to fire until he was brought down.

Fechter

The controversy that surrounded Fechter's death started then, as West Berliners stood witness to the shooting, but making things worse were the bleeding Fechter's cries for help, which lasted for a full hour before he died. People on the East German side watched as the border guards ignored the man's screams and Western guards remained in their positions. Though the East German government later issued directives for removing an injured person "directly", the reason for the new policy was "that the enemy should not be provided with any argument for getting riled up". East Germany's propaganda leader broadcast the following statement on the day of Fechter's funeral: "[W]hen this kind of element is wounded directly on the border and not retrieved immediately— then a huge fuss is made…The life of each one of our brave men in uniform is more important to us than the life of a lawbreaker. By staying away for our state border— blood, tears, and screams can be avoided."[83] Willy Brandt described the impact of Fechter's death on the people of his city: "This incident hit the Berliners hard and exacerbated their sense of outrage. Many voiced their disillusionment at the Americans' inability to help a young man who was bleeding to death".[84]

A CIA report on the construction of the Berlin Wall differentiates the approaches of the Eisenhower administration from the new Kennedy administration:"The new Kennedy administration initially made no strong policy statement in regards to Berlin, preferring to allow the Soviets to take the initiative in any provocative posturing."[85] However, some saw the building of the Berlin Wall as a somewhat welcome sign that the Soviets did not intend to challenge the United States for Berlin, at least in the near future.

For Westerners, the Berlin Wall became a place to express their freedom of thought through art and words. For East Berliners, the wall was simply *die Maurer* (the German for a walled barrier). West German Mayor Willy Brandt called it "The Wall of Shame" (*die Schandmauer*), while an American colonel living in Berlin described the existence of the wall in terms he thought Americans could relate to: "If you want to get an idea of the really important and rough effects of the wall, just imagine waking up one morning to find Manhattan divided by a wall down the middle of Fifth Avenue from the Battery to the Bronx. You live on West Tenth Street, and your office is on Park Avenue. Well, you're not going to work there anymore. Your parents live on East Eighty-second Street. You're not going to see them, and you're not going to the East Side to visit a hospital or see a movie or anything of the kind. And nobody over there is coming to see you."[86]

---

[83] Hertle, Hans. The Victims at the Berlin Wall 1961 - 1989 a Biographical Handbook. Berlin: C. Links, 2011.
[84] Large, 454.
[85] Neil C. Carmichael, Jr."A Brief History of the Crisis of the Berlin Wall: 1961". *National Declassification Center: National Records and Archives Administration.* Washington D.C.: October 27, 2001.
[86] Bainbridge, John. "Die Maurer". *The New Yorker*. October 27, 1962.

At the time of the wall's construction, the leaders of the free world were responsible for the way the world would be shaped. In an age of war-weary nations when few had the stomach to imagine a third world-wide conflict, these leaders needed to avoid another protracted war, but with the advent of nuclear weapons, there were even more serious consequences at stake, and split second decisions could lead to the deaths of hundreds of thousands of people. Winston Churchill had watched the developments in Berlin with increasing concern, and he issued a hopeful warning to the free world about the importance of finding peace through strength: "I do not believe that Soviet Russia desires war. What they desire is the fruits of war and the indefinite expansion of their power and doctrines. But what we have to consider here to-day while time remains, is the permanent prevention of war and the establishment of conditions of freedom and democracy as rapidly as possible in all countries. Our difficulties and dangers will not be removed by closing our eyes to them… What is needed is a settlement, and the longer this is delayed, the more difficult it will be and the greater our dangers will become. From what I have seen of our Russian friends and Allies during the war, I am convinced that there is nothing they admire so much as strength, and there is nothing for which they have less respect than for weakness, especially military weakness. If the Western Democracies stand together in strict adherence to the principles of the United Nations Charter, their influence for furthering those principles will be immense and no one is likely to molest them. If however they become divided or falter in their duty and if these all-important years are allowed to slip away then indeed catastrophe may overwhelm us all."

Chapter 10: 1989

In 1989, East Germany believed they were in a position to aid the struggling Soviet Union with an economic boost based on the technological advances they had been working to achieve in robotics, automation, computer design, and chemicals.[87] However, developments all across Europe were putting that economic development in jeopardy. The flight of young minds from the repressive regime was the impetus for the Wall's creation in 1961, when East Germany was witnessing a daily exodus of its young people (the brain drain) to the West. Now, 28 years later, young people were again making demands for change, an unfortunately for East Germany, what they wanted most was the freedom to leave their home country.

What was unbelievable to any who witnessed these new demands was the suddenness with which they came. As recently as February of that year, a man had been machine gunned to death while attempting to go over the wall.[88] Up until that summer of 1989, it had appeared to be business as usual at the border crossings and along the Intra-German Border which extended the separation of the two counties beyond the boundaries of Berlin.

The Soviet Union desperately needed the technological aid the East Germans could supply, but Soviet premier Mikhail Gorbachev had been unable to convince the German leader, Erich Honecker, of the need for political reform to accompany the economic growth East Germans had promised. Honecker let Gorbachev know of his lack of regard for such change, telling the general-secretary of the Eastern superpower that East Germany was well ahead of the game: "We have done our perestroika. We have nothing to restructure".[89] Honecker's chief ideologist explained that in the face of a change that seemed to be moving across Europe, each country would have to be allowed to "build its own type of socialism", not necessarily follow Moscow's lead: "Just because your neighbor wallpapers his home anew does not mean that you have to", Kurt Hager opined.[90] A comment by Soviet foreign minister Gennadi Gerasimov in October of 1989 described Soviet policy as a new and improved "Sinatra Doctrine", in which

---

[87] David M. Keithly, The Collapse of East German Communism: The Year the Wall Came Down, 1989 (Westport, CT: Praeger, 1992), 91, https://www.questia.com/read/26262339.

[88] Ibid.

[89] Tony Paterson. "Fall of the Berlin Wall: History catches up with Erich Honecker - the East German leader who praised the Iron Curtain and claimed it prevented a Third World War." *The Independent*. 29 October 2014. Web.

[90] John Borneman, After the Wall: East Meets West in the New Berlin (New York: Basic Books, 1991), 22, https://www.questia.com/read/100776334.

each of the Soviet satellites would be allowed and encouraged to make socialism "my way" in each of the countries and circumstances they faced. Just at the turn of the year in January 1989, Erich Honecker had promised that "The Wall will still be standing in 50 and even in 100 years – if the reasons for it have not been removed by then."[91] By the "reasons being removed", Honecker referred ominously to a completely Soviet dominated Berlin, something that had been on the Soviet wish list ever since World War II had ended.

Gorbachev

[91] Paterson.

Honecker

Honecker seems to have had a loose grip on the situation of Eastern Europe, though it surrounded him on all sides. A wave of change had begun sweeping through Eastern Europe, and though in the past, change had been successfully put down with violent repression by the Soviet Union, cracks were beginning to show in the superpower's armor. Whereas the Soviets had been successful in scaring revolution back into submission in East Germany, Czechoslovakia, and Hungary before, it was no longer willing or able to provide and maintain the fear with the use of actual force. In 1989, the Eastern European countries with the greatest economic problems and the weakest hardliners would experience change first.

Chapter 11: The Crumbling Bloc

Jeffrey Engle, historian and author of *The Fall of the Berlin Wall: The*

Revolutionary Legacy of 1989, explains Poland's long-term reluctance to be controlled by and put trust in the Soviet Union as a result of its history of division and lack of independence. In the 1980s, Poland's economic conditions made the country most open to reform; Poland was in great debt, experiencing very slow growth, and even food was becoming scarce.[92] A group made up of both intellectuals and unionized workers, *Solidarity*, emerged as a strong enough entity to force negotiations with the Polish government by February of 1989. Lech Walesa, Solidarity's leader, was an electrician whose influence on the brotherhood of workers he formed would affect not only Poland, but the rest of the world, too. When the first free elections in Poland were held in June, the country rejected communism and turned toward reform as a savior. [93] Just a few years before, in 1981, the Solidarity movement had been banned in Poland, but after years of declining economic growth, Poland's leaders were forced to allow Solidarity a seat at the table.[94]

---

[92] William Taubman and Svetlana Savranskaya, "Chapter 3: If a Wall Fell in Berlin and Moscow Hardly Noticed, Would It Still Make a Noise?," in The Fall of the Berlin Wall: The Revolutionary Legacy of 1989, ed. Jeffrey A. Engel (New York: Oxford University Press, 2009), 81, https://www.questia.com/read/121390201.

[93] James J. Sheehan, "Chapter 2: The Transformation of Europe and the End of the Cold War," in The Fall of the Berlin Wall: The Revolutionary Legacy of 1989, ed. Jeffrey A. Engel (New York: Oxford University Press, 2009), 54, https://www.questia.com/read/121390201.

[94] William Taubman and Svetlana Savranskaya, "Chapter 3: If a Wall Fell in Berlin and Moscow Hardly Noticed, Would It Still Make a Noise?," in The Fall of the Berlin Wall: The Revolutionary Legacy of 1989, ed. Jeffrey A. Engel (New York: Oxford University Press, 2009), 81, https://www.questia.com/read/121390201.

Walesa

The memory of the long struggle for freedom in Poland was closely linked to events in the GDR. By the time the Pope finished his visit to Warsaw in 1979, the Soviets had become largely convinced that they could no longer enforce communism on the people directly. The Soviets hoped, though, that by simply using Poland's fear of Soviet troops intervening, the effect would be quieting groups that called for reform, and Poland would see modern development of economic strength and a lack of desire for protest as a result. Solidarity was thus banned in 1981 when General Wojciech Jaruzelski instituted martial law in Poland after becoming convinced that the Soviets would intervene with bloodshed if the reform movement was not squelched. The leaders of Solidarity, including Lech Walesa, were arrested and imprisoned. Walesa foretold the future when officials came to arrest him:

"This is the moment of your defeat. These are the last nails in the coffin of communism", he said.[95]

Even in the years that have followed reunification, the Poles often struggle to forget that "[w]hen it mattered, the rise and fall of the Solidarity movement was not met with sufficient solidarity by leading politicians in Western Europe, particularly in Germany. Helmut Schmidt, the then West German Chancellor, was visiting East Germany on 13 December 1981, the day on which General Jaruzelski proclaimed martial law. Schmidt was unwilling to jeopardize the progress made in the German- German relationship under the social democratic strategy of *Ostpolitik*, even if this required a more muted response to events in Poland. Queried by West German journalists about the martial law declaration, Schmidt ended up agreeing with his host, the leader of the East German state, Erich Honecker, that Jaruzelski's radical step was necessary to preserve peace and political stability in Europe."[96]

In 1987, Pope John Paul II visited Poland and invigorated the Catholic population with calls for Solidarity to move forward and freedom to be restored. In retrospect, Timothy Garten Ash said, "I watched at close quarters John Paul II's impact on the Soviet bloc, from his election in 1978 to the collapse of the Soviet Union in 1991. No one can prove conclusively that he was a primary cause of the end of communism. However, the major figures on all sides - not just Lech Walesa, the Polish Solidarity leader, but also Solidarity's arch-opponent, General Wojciech Jaruzelski; not just the former American president George Bush Senior but also the former Soviet president Mikhail Gorbachev - now agree that he was. I would argue the historical case in three steps: without the Polish Pope, no Solidarity revolution in Poland in 1980; without Solidarity, no dramatic change in Soviet policy towards eastern Europe under Gorbachev; without that change, no velvet revolutions in 1989."[97]

---

[95] John Lewis Gaddis. The Cold War: A New History. New York: Penguin Press, 2005.
[96] Stefan Auer, "The European Union's Politics of Identity and the Legacy of 1989," Humanities Research 16, no. 3 (2010), https://www.questia.com/read/1P3-2281864101.

Walesa would become the President of Poland and continue to fight the battle against both communists and what he saw as compromisers until he finally left the Solidarity party in 2006. Under his leadership, Poland saw great economic growth, free elections, and the last Soviet troops removed from Poland. Poland's reforms and the great success that the Polish people had in bringing about change with little resistance from the Soviets were the dominoes to fall in what would become a European explosion of change.

As early as 1987, Hungary had also begun to show the rumblings of independence from the hard-liners in the communist party. Two days after Reagan's "Tear Down This Wall" appeal in West Berlin, Hungarian television began showing the speech as well as other television somewhat critical of hardliners in East Germany.[98]

Events in Hungary had given many people hope that freedom could come to Eastern Europe, though most East Germans still believed that it was a long way off for them. Hungary's communist leadership, in 1989 had been weakened to the point of agreeing to free elections to take place that June. The Hungarian communist party dissolved itself and chose a new name, the Hungarian Socialist Party.[99] According to the new party's chairman, "Uncontrolled power, the one party system, that is what made our mistakes possible…We must put an end to that. In my judgment, the new party can't be communist."[100] Though Hungary had its hard liners, most of the Hungarian Socialists had begun to believe that without abandoning communist rhetoric - and even the word socialism - they could never achieve the kind of win they needed. Poland's communist leadership still retained power, but it was sustained only by deals that allowed "a rigged electoral system…that allowed them to keep power even after a trouncing".[101]

[97] Ash, Timothy Garton. "The First World Leader." *The Guardian*. 3 April 2005.
[98] Mann 212.
[99] Barry Newman. "East Bloc Communists are Shaken by Calls for Change." *The Wall Street Journal*. 9 October 1989.
[100] Neyers qtd. in Newman, Barry.
[101] Barry Newman.

In May of 1989, Hungary opened its border with Austria but continued to check papers and refuse entry to East Germans that attempted to exit Hungary through the border. After a few months, however, Hungary tired of stemming this tide and allowed entry. The Soviet Union and Gorbachev were practically deaf to the East German government's pleas for help against the Hungarians. As Large puts it, "the Soviets… had gone out of the business of policing their shaky Eastern European Empire".[102]

As more and more East Germans sought to leave East Germany through foreign embassies in Hungary, Budapest, Warsaw, and Prague, the East German government refused to consider change. Fritz Stern calls this development proof that "the Wall had lost some of its utility, if none of its ugliness".[103] The official response to the tens of thousands of East Germans clogging the exits of all East Germany's borders? Neues Deutschland, Germany's national newspaper, said, "Through their [unpatriotic] behavior they have trampled on the moral values of the GDR and isolated themselves.... Therefore one should not cry any tears of regret at their departure."[104]

It would be difficult to deny the mass ideological movement, or as some historians have identified it, the rumblings that were making their way across Europe and, to a lesser extent, Asia in the mid-to-late 1980s. Certainly, the consequence of these ideas reaching the masses cannot be ignored by any history of the fall of the Berlin Wall. At the same time, the individuals in positions of power also had a great deal of influence over the events that would come to see the destruction of the Wall and the eventual reunification of Germany. Though modern day historians have come to largely abandon considering the role of the "great man" in history, favoring social history as the proper source for crafting the narrative and the way events play out, Fritz Stern cautions against abandoning the importance of the individual: "It has

---

[102] David Clay Large, Berlin (New York: Basic Books, 2000), 522, https://www.questia.com/read/100504423.
[103] Stern 455.
[104] Large, 522.

always seemed odd to me that in recent decades many historians have belittled the role of the individual and focused principally on the power of the 'anonymous masses'. As if Lenin and Mussolini, Gandhi and Nehru, Kemal Ataturk, Hitler, Stalin, Roosevelt, and Churchill hadn't exemplified the enormous impact a single person could have on the world stage. And here were Gorbachev, the Pope and Nelson Mandela!"[105]

Far more than Poland and Hungary, East Germany "was arguably Moscow's most important ally, possessed the strongest economy in the Soviet bloc, and ensured the continued division of Germany".[106] In his *Five Germany's I have Known*, Columbia University's former professor and Provost Fritz Stern describes his time in both East and West Germany in the late 1980s. Stern saw a serious contradiction in East German leadership's (especially that of the younger generation) desire to reform in the hopes of economic revival coupled with the ever-increasing restrictions on personal freedom and contacts with the West. The GDR had essentially survived on cash flow and help from the West, coming in the form of direct payment for the exchange of East Germany's political prisoners, as well as in the form of aid that West Germany and the larger free world gave in hopes of achieving possible reunification in the future. Erik Honecker, Stern says, had created "the paradoxical situation of the East German regime softening its position toward the West while steeling itself against reforms as practiced in the East".[107] Honecker chose to call his "success story" in East Germany "real-existing socialism". Honecker clearly believed himself a superior leader in many ways to Gorbachev, who would enter the scene long after Honecker had begun to rule.

Honecker had not only the issues of Berlin to look after but also those of larger East Germany, where the protest movement was beginning to take

[105] Stern, Fritz. Five Germany's I Have Known. New York: Farrar, Straus, and Giroux, 2006. 342.
[106] David H. Shumaker, Gorbachev and the German Question: Soviet-West German Relations, 1985-1990 (Westport, CT: Praeger Publishers, 1995), 107, https://www.questia.com/read/27983284.
[107] Stern, Fritz. Five Germany's I Have Known. New York: Farrar, Straus, and Giroux, 2006. 339.

root. The role of the Eastern European churches in the growing calls for reform and freedom should not be overlooked. While most of the church–led protests took place in Leipzig and Dresden, rather than Berlin, the movement spread its ideas throughout the country.[108] By the time of the 40th anniversary of East Germany, tensions were so high for the anticipated unrest at the upcoming 40th anniversary of the nation that the party (recalling the Tiananmen protests months earlier) had moved extra supplies of blood to Leipzig in preparation for the large protest planned there.[109]

On October 19, 1989, *The Wall Street Journal* published a story about the removal of Erich Honecker, East Germany's longtime communist leader. Honecker, some had said, sharply disagreed with Gorbachev's calls for reforms, especially because he saw them as dangerous for communism in East Germany. These observers believe that Honecker saw himself in the Stalinist mold, and held that Gorbachev should learn from him, rather than be instructed on bringing openness to East Germany.[110] In an article that appeared in *Pravda* to mark the 40th anniversary of East Germany's existence, Honecker again voiced his opposition to reforms or openness to Western influence: "Advising us to seek the benefits of socialism in a regression toward capitalism, with all its flaws, looks to us rather like saying that rain falls upward."[111]

Honecker's need to criticize Gorbachev was likely personal, but it was also rooted in fear. The reforms that Gorbachev seemed to be championing could be nothing but a threat to Honecker's regime. With East Germany's "economy in decline and close to bankruptcy…they realized they had failed to match the West's revolution in cybernetics. And, more important, they saw unrest and dissent spreading all over Eastern Europe. They were angry and afraid- and still convinced that they alone were protecting the Holy Grail."[112]

---

[108] Stern, 456.
[109] Ibid. 457.
[110] Large, 518.
[111] Honecker qtd. in Shumaker 112.
[112] Stern 442.

Honecker's replacement with Egon Krenz was quick and relatively smooth. Though Krenz came from the same background as Honecker and had championed the same communist positions (even defending the Tiananmen Square massacre committed by the communist Chinese government months before), many thought the abrupt change in power was a strong indication that the Politburo was feeling the pressure of the large demonstrations being held throughout Eastern European and in East Germany itself.

Krenz

Honecker and his wife would hold to their hard line positions until the very end of their lives. Having been helicoptered out of East Germany to safety by Gorbachev, Honecker and his wife soon found themselves housed at the Chilean embassy in the midst of Soviet unrest. From Chile in 2012, Honecker's wife gave an interview in which she continued to insist that the wall had been necessary to protect the Eastern Europeans from fascism (and the people who lost their lives attempting to escape it were only paying for their stupidity), the actions of her husband righteous and necessary, and that the saddest part of what had happened was the destruction of the great GDR: "We laid a seed in the ground which will one day come to fruition," she said, "We just didn't have enough time to realize our plans."[113] Honecker himself was sentenced to time in prison, but he was ultimately was released early for health reasons and died sometime after reaching Chile. He would also go to his grave believing that the great East German state had been on the cusp of something amazing, fettered only by the western conspirator who were those responsible for the massive desire to exit East Germany.

Chapter 12: Outside Influence

The role of Pope John Paul II in the fall of the Berlin Wall would prove significant, in large measure due to the fact he proved to be a leader that could unite many Catholics and even non-Catholics with his words of hope. He also reinvigorated the Catholic faith amongst the young wherever he went in Europe.

The Pope's initial visit to Poland in 1979 encouraged Polish Catholics to stand against communist persecution together in solidarity. So influential were his words in bringing attention to the movement that the Soviets, fearing its power, conspired to have it banned by the Polish General less than two years later. As the editor of *First Things* puts it, "He [the Pope] arrived [in Poland] on June 2, 1979, and by the time he left eight days later, 13 million Poles--more than one-third of the country's population--had seen him in person... Nearly everyone else in the nation saw him on television or heard him on the radio. The government was frightened to a hair trigger, and outside observers all had the sense that the Communist regime was doomed, one way or another, from the first moment the pope knelt down and kissed his native soil."[114]

---

[113] Connolly, Kate. "Margot Honecker defends East German dictatorship." *The Guardian.* 2 April 2012.

Angelo Codevilla was even more emphatic: "The Pope won that struggle by transcending politics. His was what Joseph Nye calls 'soft power' — the power of attraction and repulsion. He began with an enormous advantage, and exploited it to the utmost: He headed the one institution that stood for the polar opposite of the Communist way of life that the Polish people hated. He was a Pole, but beyond the regime's reach. By identifying with him, Poles would have the chance to cleanse themselves of the compromises they had to make to live under the regime. And so they came to him by the millions. They listened. He told them to be good, not to compromise themselves, to stick by one another, to be fearless, and that God is the only source of goodness, the only standard of conduct. 'Be not afraid,' he said. Millions shouted in response, 'We want God! We want God! We want God!' The regime cowered. Had the Pope chosen to turn his soft power into the hard variety, the regime might have been drowned in blood. Instead, the Pope simply led the Polish people to desert their rulers by affirming solidarity with one another. The Communists managed to hold on as despots a decade longer. But as political leaders, they were finished. Visiting his native Poland in 1979, Pope John Paul II struck what turned out to be a mortal blow to its Communist regime, to the Soviet Empire, [and] ultimately to Communism."

[114] Bottum, Joseph. "John Paul the Great." *The Weekly Standard* 10.29. 18 April 2005.

Pope John Paul II

In a second visit in 1987, John Paul II was a different man. He was returning to a Poland where less than a decade earlier, he had caused "A psychological earthquake, an opportunity for mass political catharsis..." Now, years later he had survive an assassination attempt on his life, arranged by Soviet agents as it was later confirmed. He again called on Poland to unite and called for the reinvigorating of Solidarity to right the wrongs of the past.

In "John Paul the Great", Joseph Bottum offered an assessment on the contributions of the Pope to the end of communism in Europe. Attempting to define the contributions the Pope had made, Bottum says, "You can see it perhaps most clearly in the defeat of communism--when he showed his ability to   open doors where the rest of the world saw only walls. [Many] clearly thought the only path out of the Cold War was agreement to the continuing existence of Communist regimes. This was   the lie John Paul II was never willing to tell...John Paul II's insiste[d] that communism could not survive among a people who had heard--and learned to speak--the truth about human beings' freedom, dignity, and absolute moral worth".[115]

While Fritz Stern laments the fact that the European world was astounded by the election of a Hollywood actor to the leading role of the world's most powerful country, Ronald Reagan seemed to take it all in stride. In fact, one of Reagan's most powerful weapons in dealing with the various Cold War crises that arose throughout his presidency was humor. James Mann records some of Reagan's favorite jokes, jokes that Mann describes as having a dual purpose: to lighten the mood of potentially difficult meetings between leaders on opposite sides of the philosophical table and, at the same time, to communicate his very deeply held values and positions on the failings of socialist and communist systems.[116] In 1987, West Berlin mayor Eberhard Diepgen was considering Erich Honecker's invitation to visit East Berlin, a visit the Reagan White House opposed. Preferring to communicate this opposition through an intermediary, Reagan only joked with Diepgen: "Why was Erich Honecker the last person to leave East Germany?" "...Because someone had to turn out the lights."[117]

[115] Ibid.
[116] Mann, James. The Rebellion of Ronald Reagan: A History of the End of the Cold War. New York: Viking, 2009. 144.
[117] Ibid. 145.

Reagan

  Reagan believed, as he indicated in a private letter penned in 1979 or 1980, that the West had lost their opportunity to stop the Berlin Wall during its construction in 1961: "I agree with you [he wrote to a like-minded constituent] about the lost opportunity in Berlin when we could have knocked down and prevented the completion of the wall with no hostilities following".[118] Cold War historian John Lewis Gaddis argues that it was Reagan's election that made clear to the Soviets that the option to put troops into Poland to stem the tide of Solidarity and protests no longer existed.[119]

  Though some would see his view of the Berlin Wall as simplistic or benefitting from hindsight, Reagan's idealism was clearly seen in his

---

[118] Skinner, Kiron K. et al ed. Reagan: A Life in Letters. New York: free Press, 2003. 536.
[119] Gaddis 25.

commentary on it. In June of 1987, Reagan famously stood in front of the wall and delivered a message (a message that his State Department had not expressly approved) to West and East Germans as well as to Mikhail Gorbachev himself:

"Our gathering today is being broadcast throughout Western Europe and North America. I understand that it is being seen and heard as well in the East. To those listening throughout Eastern Europe, a special word: Although I cannot be with you, I address my remarks to you just as surely as to those standing here before me. For I join you, as I join your fellow countrymen in the West, in this firm, this unalterable belief: *Es gibt nur ein Berlin*. [There is only one Berlin.]

Behind me stands a wall that encircles the free sectors of this city, part of a vast system of barriers that divides the entire continent of Europe. From the Baltic, south, those barriers cut across Germany in a gash of barbed wire, concrete, dog runs, and guard towers. Farther south, there may be no visible, no obvious wall. But there remain armed guards and checkpoints all the same--still a restriction on the right to travel, still an instrument to impose upon ordinary men and women the will of a totalitarian state. Yet it is here in Berlin where the wall emerges most clearly; here, cutting across your city, where the news photo and the television screen have imprinted this brutal division of a continent upon the mind of the world. Standing before the Brandenburg Gate, every man is a German, separated from his fellow men. Every man is a Berliner, forced to look upon a scar.

…In the 1950s, Khrushchev predicted: 'We will bury you.' But in the West today, we see a free world that has achieved a level of prosperity and well-being unprecedented in all human history. In the Communist world, we see failure, technological backwardness, declining standards of health, even want of the most basic kind--too little food. Even today, the Soviet Union still cannot feed itself. After these four decades, then, there stands before the entire world one great and inescapable conclusion: Freedom leads to prosperity. Freedom replaces the ancient hatreds among the nations with comity and peace. Freedom is the victor.

And now the Soviets themselves may, in a limited way, be coming to understand the importance of freedom... Are these the beginnings of profound changes in the Soviet state? Or are they token gestures, intended to raise false hopes in the West, or to strengthen the Soviet system without changing it? We welcome change and openness; for we believe that freedom and security go together, that the advance of human liberty can only strengthen the cause of world peace. There is one sign the Soviets can make that would be unmistakable, that would advance dramatically the cause of freedom and peace.

General Secretary Gorbachev, if you seek peace, if you seek prosperity for the Soviet Union and Eastern Europe, if you seek liberalization: Come here to this gate! Mr. Gorbachev, open this gate! Mr. Gorbachev, tear down this wall!

... In these four decades, as I have said, you Berliners have built a great city. You've done so in spite of threats--the Perhaps this gets to the root of the matter, to the most fundamental distinction of all between East and West. The totalitarian world produces backwardness because it does such violence to the spirit, thwarting the human impulse to create, to enjoy, to worship. The totalitarian world finds even symbols of love and of worship an affront. Years ago, before the East Germans began rebuilding their churches, they erected a secular structure: the television tower at Alexander Platz. Virtually ever since, the authorities have been working to correct what they view as the tower's one major flaw, treating the glass sphere at the top with paints and chemicals of every kind. Yet even today when the sun strikes that sphere--that sphere that towers over all Berlin--the light makes the sign of the cross. There in Berlin, like the city itself, symbols of love, symbols of worship, cannot be suppressed.

As I looked out a moment ago from the Reichstag, that embodiment of German unity, I noticed words crudely spray-painted upon the wall, perhaps by a young Berliner: 'This wall will fall. Beliefs become reality.' Yes, across Europe, this wall will fall. For it cannot withstand faith; it cannot withstand truth. The wall cannot withstand freedom."[120]

Reagan speaking at the Berlin Wall

[120] Ronald Reagan, "Tear Down this Wall" (Berlin, West Germany June 12, 1987).

Minutes before the speech was to begin, East Berliners could be seen gathering on the other side of the wall, straining to hear what they knew would be a message from the West. Two minutes before the speech was to begin, a loudspeaker warned, "You are asked to continue on your way. Do not remain standing".[121]

The interest of the East Berliners in hearing Reagan's words was not necessarily matched on the other side of the Atlantic. Reagan was experiencing domestic problems sparked by his popularity dip in the face of the Iran Contra scandal, and many ignored his speech or scoffed at its "naiveté". Columnist Jim Hoagland commented, "History is likely to record the challenge to tear down the wall as a meaningless taunt, delivered as a grand gesture that was not conceived as part of a coherent policy".[122] Like so many critiques of Ronald Reagan, this one makes the charge that Reagan always chose to stay in the world of grandiose ideas rather than dealing with the pragmatic. Certainly, the political commentators and even some of the members of his own administration thought, the wall would not come down in their lifetimes. It was an ugly reminder of the division of the world, but it had "saved many lives" in the sense that it was "a hell of a lot better than a war", as Kennedy had pronounced upon its construction.

Gaddis sees the Reagan contribution as critical to the American challenge to communist control of Europe. In recalling the assassination attempt on Regan's life in 1981, Gaddis notes that had it been successful, the world might be a different place: "Had Reagan's vice-president, George H.W. Bush succeeded him at that point, the Reagan presidency would have been a historical footnote…Bush, like most foreign policy experts of his generation, saw that conflict as a permanent feature of the international landscape. Reagan, like Walesa, Thatcher, Deng, and John Paul II, definitely did not".[123]

---

[121] Mann 207.
[122] Hoagland qtd. in Mann 213.
[123] Gaddis 27.

While many Germans, East and West, believed that Reagan's call to tear down the wall was unrealistic, Erich Honecker was concerned. Honecker believed that Reagan's bold words were not those of an idealistic actor but of a man who had been in dialogue with Gorbachev himself. From the point of the speech to after the wall fell, Honecker maintained his belief that the two powers had been in secret negotiations with one another to sell out East Germany. Honecker was possibly most offended not at the suggestion of tearing down the wall - a wall he believed would remain for some time to come - but at the obvious insinuation that the wall's removal was in the hands of Gorbachev and not Honecker himself.[124]

In the aftermath of the wall's fall on the night of November 9th, now former President Reagan was interviewed live by Sam Donaldson. Donaldson inquired whether when Reagan called for the wall's removal in Berlin he had thought it would come this soon. Reagan's answer was that though he had not known when, he had indeed believed that the wall would come down eventually and inevitably. He also asked Sam Donaldson for an extra moment to recall that he had heard how the East Germans had been prevented from hearing the speech by German guards. Clearly, Reagan had no regard for communist ideology, but many have held that he did have a respect and desire to work with Gorbachev, communism's leader in Europe. It was Reagan's interaction with Gorbachev, some said, that led him to believe that he could pressure the Soviet leader into making good on his claims of reform by taking down the wall that divided East from West.

Chapter 13: Officials Inside the Bloc

In 1985, less than a year after Reagan's reelection, Soviet leader Konstantin Chernenko died, leaving Mikhail Gorbachev to take his place as general-secretary. Stern calls him "a realistic Communist - if that isn't an oxymoron - he tried to see the world as it really was and not through ideological lenses".[12]

[124] Mann 210.
[125] Stern 341.

For his part, Reagan was eager for a summit with Gorbachev, having heard through his highly respected friend Margaret Thatcher that he was ready to make major changes in the communist world.

Two prevailing views of Gorbachev's role in the fall of the Berlin Wall and eventual reunification of Germany exist. In the first view, Gorbachev remained ideologically committed to communism, but in the face of so much internal unrest in the Soviet Union itself, he was content to let events happen as they may in the Soviet bloc. Thus, the events in Poland, Hungary, and East Germany, as well as the other satellite nations were not able to be controlled, and abandoned by Gorbachev for purely pragmatic reasons. In this view, though Gorbachev may have been asked for help by leaders such as Erich Honecker, he had none to give and thus hedged his bets on forging some type of relationship with the West, in what only appeared to be an ideological reverse: "Having ruled out the use of force, Moscow had no real alternative but to cut its losses and try to win whatever compensation it could from the goodwill unleashed in the West."[126]

In the second view, Gorbachev underwent genuine change. Though he at first introduced *Perestroika* and *Glasnost* as pragmatic solutions to help to preserve the communist system in Europe, over time he softened his stance and was convinced of the fact that each of the Soviet Bloc nations must choose for itself how to pursue the future. In all of this, he held out the unlikely hope that the nations, given autonomy, would choose a socialist system. Author David Shumaker champions this view in his *Gorbachev and the German Question: Soviet-West German Relations, 1985-1990.* Shumaker argues that Hungary's leaders, though desirous of encouraging a thaw, consistently communicated with Moscow, asking permission even as late as the summer of 1989 as to what to do about the thousands of East Germans fleeing the country through Hungary's borders.[127] Additionally, Shumaker

---

[126] Keep qtd. in David H. Shumaker, Gorbachev and the German Question: Soviet-West German Relations, 1985-1990 (Westport, CT: Praeger Publishers, 1995), 105, https://www.questia.com/read/27983284.

[127] David H. Shumaker, Gorbachev and the German Question: Soviet-West German Relations, 1985-1990 (Westport, CT: Praeger

notes, if the Soviet Union desired in any way to stop the crescendoing protest movement, Gorbachev could have used force or declaration of martial law to do so, even as late as 1989. Shumaker concludes, "Did the Soviet leader labor under the grand illusion of communism's inevitable triumph in Eastern Europe? Or alternatively, had Gorbachev already accepted the SED's imminent and total failure? In all likelihood, Gorbachev's reasoning lay somewhere between these two extremes."[128]

Gorbachev's openness meant that he would go so far as to entertain criticism of his East German ally from a West Germen leader, in the case of a conversation held between him and Helmut Kohl of West Germany in June of 1989. Kohl complained to Gorbachev, Now a couple of words about our mutual friends. I will tell you directly that Erich Honecker concerns me a great deal. His wife has just made a statement, in which she called on East German youth to take up arms and, if necessary, defend the achievements of socialism against external enemies. She clearly implied that socialist countries which implement reforms, stimulate democratic processes, and follow their own original road, are enemies. Primarily, she had Poland and Hungary in mind".[129]

Publishers, 1995), 105, https://www.questia.com/read/27983284.

[128] Ibid 107.

[129] William Taubman and Svetlana Savranskaya, "Chapter 3: If a Wall Fell in Berlin and Moscow Hardly Noticed, Would It Still Make a Noise?," in The Fall of the Berlin Wall: The Revolutionary Legacy of 1989, ed. Jeffrey A. Engel (New York: Oxford University Press, 2009), 85, https://www.questia.com/read/121390201.

Kohl in 1989

Just a few short and hectic months later, Gorbachev would head to East Germany to visit his and Chancellor Kohl's "mutual friends". On October 6-7, 1989, East Berlin was to celebrate the 40th anniversary of the founding of the East German state, but security and surveillance by the Stasi had been increased heavily in response to Honecker's concerns that the visit of the Soviet leader, Gorbachev could cause unrest in the city. Gorbachev's very controlled visit did spark local protests, though he did not openly call for reform in a way that would make the East German leadership uncomfortable. He did, however, in his meeting with the leaders of the Socialist party give a warning that "one cannot overlook signals of reality. Life punishes those who arrive too late. We have learned this from our development".[130] Shumaker argues, though, that Gorbachev did the most he could to make the point that he supported national sovereignty: "During his stay in East Berlin for the 40th anniversary of the East German state, Gorbachev publicly stressed that 'in each country the people will determine what they need and what to do'."[131]

---

[130] Gorbachev qtd. in Shumaker 112.

[131] Ibid 106.

Behind the scenes, Honecker defended his hard line attitude to Gorbachev, reminding him that the East Germans boasted a higher standard of living than the citizens of the Soviet Union. If East Germany lost the ability to retain its young people, Honecker warned, East Germany's reputation and her high-tech generation would be lost to unrest and exodus.

According to Valery Boldin, a former Gorbachev aide, when Gorbachev returned from East Germany, he "announced that Honecker's days were numbered and that we should start thinking about the reunification of Germany".[132] On October 16th, Egon Krenz and two other East German leaders, Willi Stoph and Erich Mielke, wrote to Moscow seeking Gorbachev's permission to replace Honecker as leader. Honecker would be removed from office only a few days later.[133]

Observers in the Soviet Union described Gorbachev's approach to the situation in Europe as "ad hoc". According to observers, Gorbachev and his minister of Soviet affairs were "[a]ble but inexperienced, impatient to reach agreement, but excessively self-assured and flattered by the Western media… often outwitted and outplayed by their Western partners".[134] History records no direct comment on the fall of the wall by Gorbachev, whose own aides found him unable to be reached by phone on the night of November 9th. That said, in 2009, 20 years after the Wall fell Gorbachev did make comments to Western reporters about the Berlin Wall: "If the Soviet Union did not want [the wall to fall], nothing would have happened, not any kind of unification." When asked what the alternative would be, Gorbachev answered, "I don't know, maybe a World War III…I am very proud of the decision we made. The wall did not simply fall, it was destroyed, just as the Soviet Union was destroyed…The fall of the Berlin Wall was a synthesized indication of what was going on in the world and where it was heading to. My policy was open

[132] Valery Boldin, Ten Years That Shook the World: The Gorbachev Era as Witnessed by His Chief of Staff, trans. Evelyn Rossiter (New York: Basic Books, 1994), 143,
[133] Large, 525.
[134] Vladislav M. Zubok, A Failed Empire: The Soviet Union in the Cold War from Stalin to Gorbachev (Chapel Hill, NC: University of North Carolina Press, 2007), 327,

and sincere, a policy aimed at using democracy and not spilling blood, but this cost me very [dearly], I can tell you that."[135]

Gorbachev preferred to see the events that unfolded in the Soviet Union and Eastern Europe as ultimately the choice of the choice of the people — even as a choice he may have disagreed with. By the time 20 years had passed, Gorbachev preferred to see himself not as trying to retain power in the Soviet Union by minimizing unrest in his satellites but rather as wise guide for the masses who had decided on democratic action, ensuring that the transition would take place in relative peace and without violence.

When Gorbachev decided it was time for Honecker to exit the scene, the Politburo had already decided on his replacement, a younger man, to be sure, but a man embroiled in the same fight as his unfortunate predecessor. Egon Krenz had grown up in the Soviet system, attending college and becoming known as the "crown prince" of the GDR for his faithfulness in matters of party security .[136] He replaced his mentor and friend Honecker, the man he called his "foster father and political teacher", after betraying him and voting for his ouster in the midst of Honecker's disagreements with the Soviets and failures to control the burgeoning protest movement in East Germany. Krenz, however, did not have the trust of the people any more than Honecker had at the end of his rule. An exiled East German said Krenz was "a walking invitation to flee the republic".[137] Stern calls Krenz "a less doctrinaire functionary [than Honecker] mouthing vague notions of reform".[138]

Krenz, who unluckily received the ailing Honecker's "blessing" upon his exit, proved paralyzed and unable to deal with the demands for reform. Krenz lost popularity by taking over not only as the Socialist party leader but also as head of state, the same position which Honecker had occupied.[139]

---

[135] Marquardt, Alexander. "Gorbachev: The Man Who Prevented World War III?" *ABC News.com.* 8 November 2009.
[136] Dennis Kavanagh, ed., A Dictionary of Political Biography (Oxford: Oxford University Press, 1998), 276, https://www.questia.com
[137] Ibid. 526.
[138] Stern 457.
[139] Kavanagh 276.

Despite Krenz's desperate attempts to placate reformers in East Germany, his promises proved too little, too late. He was seen as nothing more than Honecker "with a gallbladder", as the joke went. The number of protestors in Leipzig grew during Krenz's first six weeks in power from 70,000 to over half a million, and Krenz opened the borders with Czechoslovakia on the advice of the Soviets only after he revealed to Gorbachev the extreme amount of debt East Germany had incurred with the West. Krenz and Gorbachev knew they would need to build good will with the West in order to make the payments necessary for the GR to survive.[140]

In the face of the mass exodus of Germans that followed Shabowski's botched press conference explaining the new travel rules for East Germans, Krenz refused to give shoot to kill orders against the people. He was ousted from power on December 3, 1989, less than two months after his betrayal of Honecker.[141]

Chapter 14: November 9, 1989

In the months that led to the fall of the Berlin Wall, pubic protest grew almost daily, and after so many years of repression by Stasi agents, many Germans participating were surprised at the fact that demonstrations were allowed to move forward. Though many demonstrators were subject to beatings and arrest, the crowds gathering in Eastern churches grew each week. "Demonstrators in Leipzig and other cities proclaimed popular sovereignty with the slogan 'Wir sind das Volk', or 'We are the People'", reported John Leslie, a student interning with the NBC nightly news program in Leipzig and other eastern cities. This phrase would later morph to "We are one people" as Easterners grew bolder to challenge the Socialist government's claims to being the People's Republic and the crowds desired to identify themselves more boldly.[142]

---

[140] Vladislav M. Zubok, A Failed Empire: The Soviet Union in the Cold War from Stalin to Gorbachev (Chapel Hill, NC: University of North Carolina Press, 2007), 326

[141] Ibid.

[142] John Leslie, "The Fall of the Berlin Wall Twenty Years Later: John Leslie Provides Remembrances of 1989 from Inside East Germany," New Zealand International Review 34, no. 5 (2009), https://www.questia.com/read/1G1-207943787.

Only a few months before the fall of the Wall, John Leslie was invited to be a part of a discussion between East German officials and their West German guests. At the event, one of the party secretaries was asked for his thoughts on the repercussions of East German youth being able to witness the stirring revolutions in Poland, Hungary, and the Soviet Union on television. The secretary replied first to the East German student who was translating for the English speaking students: "Too many of our citizens spend too much time watching television and not enough time building socialism!" At this point the Cambridge-educated East German translator remarked that she saw the response as "ideological, heavy-handed and defensive". This is another illustration of the disconnect that existed between East German youth and those in East Germany who were old enough to have been convinced that the harsh repression and lack of freedom were at worst inevitable and at best protection against the Western fascists who could otherwise overtake them.[143]

Though the peaceful demonstrations in Berlin were not ended in a Tiananmen-style crackdown, the Stasi made sure that the protestors felt their presence. Stasi police were stationed outside of the churches to intercept those protestors who exited. Those deemed "guilty" of incitement, speaking against the state, or other "crimes" were taken to be interrogated, had their names and pictures recorded, and were humiliated in various states of undress as the Stasi force them to sign statements incriminating themselves.[144]

In the years following the fall of the Berlin Wall, many writers have taken the time to analyze the event chronologically. Just how did the messages about the easing of travel restrictions get to the people? What was the East German government's intention versus how was it implemented by the people who carried it out? Before attempting an answer to these questions, it is important to note that the fall of the Berlin Wall was in no way inevitable, at least in the sense of when and how it took place. Timothy Garten Ash

---

[143] Ibid.
[144] Borneman 23.

cautions his *Guardian* readers regarding the tendency to view it this way, writing that "it is almost impossible to recreate the emotional intensity of the moment of liberation. For that intensity came from having lived for most, if not all, your life with the aching certainty that something like this was, precisely, impossible".[145]

In another warning to readers who assume the fall of the wall was simply a foregone conclusion, historian David Clay Large reminds his readers that East Germany and its leaders had perhaps the least reason to believe they were in danger. Honecker, Large claims, had a great amount of credibility as the head of Germany since the end of World War II, and had done a very effective job at squelching dissidence. As had been the practice of East Germany since the construction of the Berlin Wall and the accompanying economic struggles, dissidents could become prisoners, who would then become saleable goods to West Germany.[146] The severity of response to those who desired escape and the internal intimidation of East Germans in their workplaces, homes, and even churches gave many Germans reason enough to believe that they would live and die in the shadow of the wall. After 28 years, there were now many living who had never known a day without it.

In the end, however, the pressure mounted on even East Germany to make concessions. Though Honecker disagreed with Gorbachev's reform attempts, it was still difficult when "GDR authorities found themselves in the awkward position of trying to curtail contacts between East German citizens and the mother country of communism".[147] The people of East Germany had limited chances for public gatherings without strict control. In January of 1988, East German leaders had gathered to honor the communist radical Rosa Luxemburg. When a number of protestors displayed a banner with a quote from the communist heroine ("True Freedom is Always the Freedom of the

---

[145] Timothy Garten Ash. "The Fall of the Berlin Wall: What it Meant to Be There." The Guardian. 6 November 2014. Web.
[146] Large 520.
[147] Ibid.

Non-conformists"), they were immediately arrested and exiled from the country.[148]

Finally, tensions between East Germany and her resentful neighbors had reached a breaking point. With literally tens of thousands of East German refugees clogging the streets, highways, and embassies of her neighbor nations, it was up to East Germany to ease travel restrictions and make some concessions to stem the tide, so the decision was made to allow travel outside of East Berlin for one month to those with proper passports. Large notes that the number of East Germans with proper passports was so low that this would not have caused a high influx of travel outside of the borders. However, the hastily called press conference and the rewriting of the policy up to the last hour meant that a mistake would be made that would change the world as the Germans knew it.

Guenter Schabowski was the official spokesperson at a press conference that was being televised live throughout East Germany. Charged with delivering the new travel guidelines in a hastily-called press conference, Schabowski began his remarks: "You see, comrades, I was informed today...that such an announcement had been...distributed earlier today. You should actually have it already...1) 'Applications for travel abroad by private individuals can now be made without the previously existing requirements (of demonstrating a need to travel or proving familial relationships). The travel authorizations will be issued within a short time. Grounds for denial will only be applied in particular exceptional cases. The responsible departments of passport and registration control in the People's Police district offices in the GDR are instructed to issue visas for permanent exit without delays and without presentation of the existing requirements for permanent exit.'""

After being asked when it would come into effect, Schabowski replied,

---

[148] Large, 520.

"That comes into effect, according to my information, immediately, without delay." When asked if it also applies for West Berlin, he responded, "Permanent exit can take place via all border crossings from the GDR to the FRG and West Berlin, respectively."[149]

Picture of the press conference

The Wall Street Journal speculated that Schabowski had faltered not because he had not prepared carefully enough, as some charged, but because he was "not used to scrutiny by a free press…[And] he couldn't deal with rapid-fire questions from international journalists".[150] Whatever the real cause of Schabowski's struggle to communicate, it became immediately clear that "seeming accidents have the power to shape history".[151] Later, American journalist Tom Brokaw would recall following Schakowsky upstairs after the conference had concluded and asking him to re-read the portion of the brief that lifted the travel restrictions on border crossings between East and West

[149] Guenter Schabowski, "Guenter Schabowski's Press Conference in the GDR International Press Center," Making the History of 1989, Item #449, http://chnm.gmu.edu/1989/items/show/449 (accessed February 27 2015, 8:28 pm).
[150] Walker, Marcus. "Did Journalists' Questions Topple the Berlin Wall?" The Wall Street Journal. 7 November 2014.
[151] Stern 459.

Berlin directly. It was then, Brokaw realized, that the end of the Berlin Wall had come. In his newscast, he told the watching world, "This is a historic night…. The East German Government has just declared that East German citizens will be able to cross the wall … without restrictions."[152] Schabowski would be expelled from the party but fail to escape prosecution as a high Politburo official; he served only a few months of a three-year sentence after distancing himself from communist ideals.

On the evening of November 9th, 1989, Harald Jaeger, an East German border guard, watched a television as he ate a meal at the canteen before arriving for his guard duty shift at the Berlin Wall that night at 6:00 p.m. Hearing the removal of travel restrictions would take place "immediately", he remembers "almost choking on my bread roll". He arrived at the wall to find other skeptical guards and made multiple telephone calls to his superiors, attempting to get clarification about what to do with the now gathering crowds. At first, Jaeger's superiors simply ignored his question, telling them to send people without authorization home. After realizing the seriousness of the situation, however, Jaeger was instructed to let the "most agitated" members of the crowd pass through to West Berlin in hopes of appeasing them. Obviously, the opposite effect was achieved and Jaeger had no further instruction from his superiors. Fearing for the safety of the burgeoning crowd, Jaeger delivered the order to open the border between East and West Berlin at 11:30 p.m.[153] Thus, Jaeger is most often credited with being the man who actually "took down" the Wall.

Another East German border guard, Erich Wittman, recalled his memory of the evening: "I was promoted to Corporal, and was directly posted as the Officer of the main checkpoint of the Berlin wall. I still remember the tensions, thousands of cars was in front of me, honking and wanted me to move, which I refused….The news of the Berlin wall being open for anyone

[152] Melvyn P. Leffler, "Chapter 5: Dreams of Freedom, Temptations of Power," in The Fall of the Berlin Wall: The Revolutionary Legacy of 1989, ed. Jeffrey A. Engel (New York: Oxford University Press, 2009), 136,
[153] "Former border guard Harald Jaeger recalls how he opened the Berlin Wall." South China Morning Post. 6 November 2014.

hadn't reached us who were posted at the wall, only when my girlfriend, who I for the first time on [sic] months seen, came to me and told me about it. I was in shock and didn't know what to do, all around me, thousands of people started to gather around me, climbing over the wall, some even brought tools and sledge-hammers and started to destroy the wall, the people kept yelling at us as we told them to stay back, then…On the TV, which I saw through the window of the Guard's Resting place, I could see the politicians ordering the opening to West Berlin for everyone, I ordered the soldiers to open the gates and let the cars pass, the yells formed into cheers and all over us, people came to hug me and my men, and the cars kept swarming over the border. Erika grabbed onto my uniform, and pulled me to her, and hugged me, I responded in kissing her, then a camera man appeared on the scene and filmed the opening of the wall, and got us on tape…The supreme officer came to me later, asked me why the people are flooding over to West Germany, I told him. The German Democratic Republic is dead, they announced it on Television, open your borders as well for these people. He quickly went away, and all over East Germany the news came, and the Berlin wall was flooded by people over several days."

A crane removing pieces of the wall in December 1989

Pictures of East Germans talking to West Germans through the wall in late November 1989

1990 picture of the graffiti and pieces of the wall chipped away

In 2009, the New York Times commemorated the night of the Berlin Wall's fall with a gathering of remembrances of the days and nights that changed the world:

- Susan Prediger remembers: "We had trouble that day purchasing the hammer and the chisel -- everyone was buying them up all around the city. The ringing from the hammers all along the wall was deafening, our hands were cold, but we were all elated...I could never have imagined that eventually the East, where we had trouble finding ways to spend the money we were forced to exchange, would one day be my home".[154]

[154] Jon Huang, et al. "The View from the Wall." *The New York Times*. 6 November 2009.

- Marc Farre remembers: "…We had been to the Wall the day before, and heard the distant sound of East German then-leader Egon Krenz trying to calm the crowd at a speech over on Alexanderplatz, I had no knowledge that anything unusual was happening that evening of November 9. Suddenly the phone rang in the apartment. .. an excited voice shouting out 'Did you hear?! Did you see?!'…I looked out the window and saw, intermingled with the Mercedes and Audis of West Berlin, the unmistakable sight (and smell) of dozens of Trabants -- those little, grey bread-box cars mass-produced somewhere in the Eastern Bloc. My friend and I rushed over to Checkpoint Charlie, the spot where we'd been the day before. As we approached the Wall, we could hear the sounds of bongos and shouting and screaming. People had just started scaling the Wall, and we enthusiastically jumped up, helped by others. We climbed back down [from the wall] and joined the crowds that had swarmed the suddenly opened Checkpoint Charlie, taking our positions on either side of the 'receiving line' -- banging on the tops of these papier-mâché cars, hugging people, dispensing chocolates…It was the most extraordinary experience of my life. The kind of coming together of strangers that usually requires a horrific tragedy was made possible instead that night by the abrupt release from a multi-decade, slow-burning tragedy".

- Anke Domscheit Berg, 21-year-old resident of East Berlin, recorded in her diary, November 9th 1989: "Hours ago, the news came in - the border of the German Democratic Republic has been opened. Unbelievable. Every hour, 3,500 people are leaving the country. The Democratic Awakening stood in front of the crossing point and tried to persuade people to stay. To so many people, everything is falling apart. There are resignations all the time; everything has been turned upside down. To America in the summer? Can I pay for the ticket? Visiting

France? The Mediterranean Sea, Holland, Tunisia, Luanda? How can I have a holiday, where can I find the money? I am longing for everywhere, only to return."

And again, on 13 November, 1989: "…everyone can cross over as they like. Unbelievable… Set off early on Saturday by car to the new crossing at Bernauerstrasse-Brunnenstrasse. Dad pushed his way through. We were standing for an hour, the queue was endless, it was moving forwards all the time. We only needed to raise up our ID. All around were broken walls, construction workers and border patrols. I beamed at one of them - even they are happy now, despite the stress. Youths from West Berlin were sitting on the wall, clapping and waving. I had tears in my eyes. Everywhere West Berliners, laughing and waving…"[155]

---

[155] "Young Woman's Berlin Wall Diary Revealed." Ee.co.uk 8 November 2014.

Picture of a man juggling on the wall in November 1989

A picture taken in 1990

Chapter 15: Reactions to the Fall of the Wall

A foreign correspondent in Germany at the time of the wall's fall noted that while young people in France were excited by the possibilities of a united Germany, some French political observers greatly feared a resurgent Germany. In an interview with the Hampton Roads International Security Quarterly, Wickert argues that many Germans had not looked for the fall of the wall to occur because they believed their separation was a punishment for the atrocities committed by many Germans during World War II.[156] In addition, the transition to a united nation was not an easy one for the German people. David Clay Large, author of *Berlin*, explains that Berlin "emerged as a microcosm of the famous 'Wall in the Head'—that amalgam of social,

---

[156] "The Fall of the Berlin Wall Is Part of My Biography"" Hampton Roads International Security Quarterly, October 1, 2009, https://www.questia.com/read/1P2-20930958.

political, cultural, and psychological barriers that replaced the old concrete wall in keeping eastern and western Germans apart".[157]

An interview with a teacher from Dresden revealed that a number of East Germans, in some way, missed their days in "Egypt" – when the safety net of European-style socialism meant that though the standard of living was rather low, it was steady. However, the teacher rejected this brand of nostalgia: "What matters is that I can talk with an American journalist without going to jail, that I can travel without filling out forms, that I can read what I want to read, that I'm not told what TV station I can watch and not watch, that at school I don't have to say something that I don't say in private at home. This is what is decisive to me today."[158]

Margaret Thatcher, in an interview outside 10 Downing Street, warned that talk of German reunification was much, much "too fast" and that East Germany would be required to show its development as a democracy before that could be taken under serious consideration. Despite issuing cautions about the pace at which reunification should take place and the idea that it was impossible for all East Germans to leave the country[159], Thatcher did take a moment to delight in the historical moment: "I think it is a great day for freedom. I watched the scenes on television last night and again this morning because I felt one ought not only hear about them but see them because you see the joy on people's faces and you see what freedom means to them; it makes you realize that you cannot stifle or suppress people's desire for liberty and so I watched with the same joy as everyone else."[160]

Thatcher mentioned that she looked forward to discussing the event and its fallout with President George H.W. Bush in the near future. President Bush, successor to the years of Regan idealism, seemed low key to many in his response to the news of the wall's fall. He responded that he "was not an

[157] David Clay Large, Berlin (New York: Basic Books, 2000), https://www.questia.com/read/100504423
[158] Packer, George. "November 9th." The New Yorker. 16 November 2009.
[159] Thatcher, Margaret. "Remarks on the Berlin Wall (fall thereof)". Thatcher Archive: COI transcript. 10 November 1989.
[160] Ibid.

emotional kind of guy", but many of his advisors believed the same thing that Bush, a former member of the State Department, also believed: caution in dealing with Gorbachev, the Soviets and Eastern Europe was necessary. Bush's Secretary of Defense, Dick Cheney, warned, "We must guard against gambling our nation's security on what may be a temporary aberration in the behavior of our foremost adversary."[161]

On Christmas day in 1989, Leonard Bernstein conducted musicians from both east and west at the site of the now defunct wall.[162] In performing "Ode to Joy", Bernstein took the liberty of replacing the German word for Joy with a similar word for "freedom", the freedom that could now be celebrated by both Eastern and Western musicians simultaneously.

Vera Pavlova, an internationally acclaimed poet born in Moscow, wrote of the wall that divided Berlin and contrasted the toll that it took on so many with the "day like any other day" feeling of November 9, 1989. Here is her poem "It Was A Weird Wall":

> "It was a weird wall
>
> Like the Mobius strip,
>
> it had only one side,
>
> the other one was unseen:
>
> the far side of the Moon.
>
> But some people would race
>
> against bullets, to rip
>
> the barbed finish tape

[161] Melvyn P. Leffler, "Chapter 5: Dreams of Freedom, Temptations of Power," in The Fall of the Berlin Wall: The Revolutionary Legacy of 1989, ed. Jeffrey A. Engel (New York: Oxford University Press, 2009), 137,
[162] Stern 460.

with their chests, to give

a push to the wrecking ball:

the pendulum of the invisible clock.

Under 11/09/89,

my diary says:

'Natasha lost a front tooth,

Liza for the first time

stood up in her crib

on her own.'"

Though West German leader Helmut Kohl predicted that the reunification of Germany (a shocking idea in those early days) would take place over a period of 10 years, the reunification process would be driven not by the politicians but by the people. The free elections that took place in East Germany had been expected to return support for the now moderated socialist party, but the East Germans voted instead for rapid reunification with the West and democratic government: "Most East Germans were tired of socialist Promises and practices, they wanted an end to experiments, and they wanted what they imagined the other Germans had. The proletariat wanted the fruits of capitalism - and they wanted them immediately. Forty years of deprivation had been enough".[163]

Despite the cautions of Margaret Thatcher and others, the reunification of Germany happened with lightning speed. While many predicted it would take a decade to bring the two nations together, the East Germans decidedly

[163] Stern 465.

rejected the socialist legacy and the two countries were made one on October 3, 1990, less than a year after that fateful, accidental night of November 9, 1989. West Germany's constitution served as the united Germany's governing document, and the country's first elections were held that December.

In the meantime, the interim period revealed much about the conditions in East Germany compared with the West, as well as the fact that East Germany's former leaders had been living in the very luxuries they called the trappings of capitalism. The revelations of the Stasi practices and the discovery of millions of files that the secret police had kept on East Germans citizens added to this rejection of any further dealings with Socialist politics.[16]

In his contribution to a larger work on the fall of the Wall, Melvyn Leffler writes that Americans saw the fall of the wall as "the conquest of freedom over tyranny, the liberation of a people, the redemptive role of the United States of America. It confirmed the utility of power, the correctness of containment, the universal appeal of freedom, the triumph of good over evil. It foreshadowed the temptation to use power anew, when great threat appeared, in order to defeat a new devil and to fulfill God's intention for all men to be free".[165]

As 1990 wore on, historians, archaeologists, and museum curators began to bemoan the chipping away of the physical wall as detrimental not only to history but to the political processes of the future Germany. Some expressed concern that if the wall was removed in its totality, it was also easier to forget the years of oppression and curtailing of rights that had come with it. There were also former East Germans affronted by what they saw as perhaps the jocular nature of obtaining one's own piece of a wall that for them had meant so much pain. While stalls selling pieces of the wall were set up almost

---

[164] Stern 463.
[165] Melvyn P. Leffler, "Chapter 5: Dreams of Freedom, Temptations of Power," in The Fall of the Berlin Wall: The Revolutionary Legacy of 1989, ed. Jeffrey A. Engel (New York: Oxford University Press, 2009), 133,

immediately throughout West Berlin (the owners of which quickly found that colorful pieces from the West Berlin side were the better sellers), many East Germans believed that an element of sobriety was missing from the crumbling wall's end.[166]

In 1990 and 1991, Gorbachev tried to preserve the Soviet Union in a less centralized form that would grant some form of home rule to the Soviet republics. However, in 1991, Soviet hardliners began to organize a coup against Gorbachev, who they saw as responsible for the rapid deterioration of the Soviet Union and its communist allies in Eastern Europe. The coup plotters executed their plan in August 1991, attempting to confine Gorbachev to his summer residence and restore the supremacy of the Communist Party. Boris Yeltsin, one of Gorbachev's top aides, organized popular resistance to the coup and ultimately defeated it.

In the months after the coup, 10 former Soviet republics declared their independence. Russia, long the dominant member of the Soviet Union, followed on December 12, 1991. Within two weeks, the Soviet Union would be officially dissolved.

Today, pieces of the Berlin Wall have been spread all over the world, and almost as soon as the wall came down, interest in its pieces became a phenomenon. Individuals in the United States, according to a journal article in CLIO, were the biggest market. A Canadian in Berlin on the night of November 9th recalled, "I knew everybody in the world was watching history happening here and that's when I got the idea. I figured people would love to have a piece of that history, too. So I bought a hammer and chisel and started knocking off pieces of the Wall to sell back home".[167] Loshitzky, the author of the piece, expresses great concern, even disdain, for what she calls the "commodification of history", citing what she deems the shallow and

---

[166] Frederick Baker, "The Berlin Wall: Production, Preservation and Consumption of a 20th-Century Monument," Antiquity 67, no. 257 (1993), https://www.questia.com/read/1G1-15143722.

[167] Yosefa Loshitzky, "Constructing and Deconstructing the Wall," CLIO 26, no. 3 (1997), https://www.questia.com/read/1G1-19984489.

untimely Checkpoint Charlie Museum in Berlin as well as the escape tunnel turned escape museum that runs under what was once a divided city.

Collectors' enthusiasm hasn't been dampened by such critique. Today, parts of the wall can be found on 6 continents, and pieces are on display throughout Germany, in American presidential libraries, at Westminster College in Fulton, Missouri (the site of Winston Churchill's Iron Curtain speech), in parks and museums around the world, at military bases, and even in American theme parks and casinos.

The wall that was built first as a test of Western resolve and later strengthened after the West's lack of response had divided the country of Germany for 28 years. As some historians see it, the failure to respond to the initial test of the Soviets and East Germans led to many more years of testing and a war of words over the divided city, which itself was a symbol of a divided world. For all the wall could do to the lives, fortunes, and spiritual states of those living in the East, it could never take their desire for freedom away completely. Many world leaders, directly involved in the aftermath of the Berlin Wall's construction in 1961, can attest to the fact that in keeping their people contained inside an "anti-Fascist Protection Rampart," the Soviets fooled no one. The wall crushed the spirit of the people, but it never fully destroyed it. In thousands of escape attempts, some resulting in the earning of freedom and many ending with death or arrest, the attempts to leave a place that would not allow one to be free continued all the way to the night the wall was opened. Leaving East Germany, even in the hectic days preceding the fall of the wall, required strength and determination, and ultimately a desire for freedom above safety. In Honecker's desperate last attempts at control, he allowed one trainload of East Germans to pass into the West in an attempt to alleviate the congestion that was now all too obvious to the rest of the world. The condition Honecker offered was that in the passing of the train, all passengers' names and contact information would be recorded. A country with a history of secret police activity and persecution of family and associates could not be taken lightly, even when one was on their way across the border.

On the 20th anniversary of the fall of the Wall, British Prime Minister Gordon Brown said, "The wall that had imprisoned half a city, half a country, half a continent, half a world for nearly a third of a century was swept away by the greatest force of all - the unbreakable spirit of men and women who dared to dream in the darkness, who knew that while force has the temporary power to dictate, it can never ultimately decide."

It is in this spirit that those who remember the wall can hold out hope against the forces that today attempt to keep people in darkness and fear.

Bibliography

Ash, Timothy Garten. "The Fall of the Berlin Wall: What it Meant to Be There." *The Guardian*. 6 November 2014. Web.

Ash, Timothy Garten. "The First World Leader. " *The Guardian*. 3 April 2005.

Auer, Stefan, "The European Union's Politics of Identity and the Legacy of 1989," *Humanities Research* 16, no. 3 (2010), https://www.questia.com/read/1P3-2281864101.

Baker, Frederick. "The Berlin Wall: Production, Preservation and Consumption of a 20th-Century Monument," *Antiquity* 67, no. 257 (1993), https://www.questia.com/read/1G1-15143722.

Boldin, Valery. *Ten Years That Shook the World: The Gorbachev Era as Witnessed by His Chief of Staff*, trans. Evelyn Rossiter (New York: Basic Books, 1994).

Borneman, John. *After the Wall: East Meets West in the New Berlin* (New York: Basic Books, 1991), 22, https://www.questia.com/read/100776334.

Bottum, Joseph. "John Paul the Great." *The Weekly Standard* 10.29. 18 April 2005.

Connolly, Kate. "Margot Honecker Defends East German Dictatorship." *The Guardian.* 2 April 2012.

"The Fall of the Berlin Wall Is Part of My Biography." *Hampton Roads International Security Quarterly*, October 1, 2009, https://www.questia.com/read/1P2-20930958.

"Former Border Guard Harald Jaeger Recalls How He Opened the Berlin Wall." *South China Morning Post.* 6 November 2014.

Gaddis, John Lewis. *The Cold War: A New History.* New York: Penguin Press, 2005.

Huang, Jon. et al. "The View from the Wall." The New York Times. 6 November 2009.

Kavanagh, Dennis ed., *A Dictionary of Political Biography* (Oxford: Oxford University Press, 1998), 276, https://www.questia.com

Keithly, David M. *The Collapse of East German Communism: The Year the Wall Came Down, 1989* (Westport, CT: Praeger, 1992) https://www.questia.com/read/26262339.

Large, David Clay. *Berlin* (New York: Basic Books, 2000), 522.https://www.questia.com/read/100504423.

Leffler, Melvyn P. "Chapter 5: Dreams of Freedom, Temptations of Power," in *The Fall of the Berlin Wall: The Revolutionary Legacy of 1989*, ed. Jeffrey A. Engel (New York: Oxford University Press, 2009).

Leslie, John "The Fall of the Berlin Wall Twenty Years Later: John Leslie Provides Remembrances of 1989 from Inside East Germany," New Zealand International Review 34, no. 5 (2009), https://www.questia.com/read/1G1-207943787.

Loshitzky, Yosefa."Constructing and Deconstructing the Wall," CLIO 26, no. 3 (1997), https://www.questia.com/read/1G1-19984489.

Mann, James. *The Rebellion of Ronald Reagan: A History of the End of the Cold War.* New York: Viking, 2009.

Marquardt, Alexander. "Gorbachev: The Man Who Prevented World War III?" *ABC News.com.* 8 November 2009.

Newman, Barry. "East Bloc Communists are Shaken by Calls for Change*." The Wall Street Journal.* 9 October 1989.

Packer, George. "November 9th." *The New Yorker.* 16 November 2009.

Paterson, Tony. "Fall of the Berlin Wall: History catches up with Erich Honecker - the East German leader who praised the Iron Curtain and claimed it prevented a Third World War." *The Independent.* 29 October 2014.Web.

Ronald Reagan, "Tear Down this Wall" (Berlin, West Germany June 12, 1987).

Schabowski, Guenter. "Guenter Schabowski's Press Conference in the GDR International Press Center," *Making the History of 1989*, Item #449, http://chnm.gmu.edu/1989/items/show/449 (accessed February 27 2015, 8:28 pm).

Sheehan, James J. "Chapter 2: The Transformation of Europe and the End of the Cold War," in *The Fall of the Berlin Wall: The Revolutionary Legacy of 1989*, ed. Jeffrey A. Engel (New York: Oxford University Press, 2009), 54, https://www.questia.com/read/121390201.

Shumaker, David H. *Gorbachev and the German Question: Soviet-*

West German Relations, 1985-1990 (Westport, CT: Praeger Publishers, 1995), 107, https://www.questia.com/read/27983284.

Skinner, Kiron K. et al ed. *Reagan: A Life in Letters*. New York: free Press, 2003. 536.

Stern, Fritz. *Five Germanys I Have Known*. New York: Farrar, Straus, and Giroux, 2006.

Taubman, William and Svetlana Savranskaya. "Chapter 3: If a Wall Fell in Berlin and Moscow Hardly Noticed, Would It Still Make a Noise?," in *The Fall of the Berlin Wall: The Revolutionary Legacy of 1989*, ed. Jeffrey A. Engel (New York: Oxford University Press, 2009), https://www.questia.com/read/121390201.

Thatcher, Margaret. "Remarks on the Berlin Wall (fall thereof)". *Thatcher Archive*: COI transcript. 10 November 1989.

Walker, Marcus. "Did Journalists' Questions Topple the Berlin Wall?" *The Wall Street Journal*. 7 November 2014.

"Young Woman's Berlin Wall Diary Revealed." *Ee.co.uk* 8 November 2014.

Zubok, Vladislav M. A Failed Empire: The Soviet Union in the Cold War from Stalin to Gorbachev (Chapel Hill, NC: University of North Carolina Press, 2007).